When Destiny Calls
Trouble Answers

Pastor Vendrix Headley

Written Words Publishing LLC
14189 E Dickinson Drive, Unit F
Aurora, Colorado 80014
www.writtenwordspublishing.com

Published by Written Word Publishing LLC September 1, 2023.

ISBN: 978-1-961610-09-5 (paperback)
ISBN: 978-1-961610-10-1 (eBook)

Library of Congress Control Number: 2023915394

Manufactured and printed in the United States of America

DEDICATION

I am filled with gratitude and humility as I dedicate this book to God Almighty for being my calm during the storm.

I also dedicate this book to my amazing sons, Aniel and Nashon Headley, who have been a constant source of support and love on my journey towards my destiny. Through the highs and lows, they have been my unwavering companions, giving me the strength I needed when I needed it the most. Their steadfast faith and resilience have genuinely inspired me.

Additionally, I dedicate this book to my extraordinary friends who have uplifted me during challenging times with their positivity and firm smiles. Despite their trials, they have remained resolute in pursuing joy and fulfilment. Their courage and determination are remarkable and inspirational for all who know them.

To all those who are struggling to find their way on the path to destiny, this book is for you. Whether facing seemingly insurmountable challenges or feeling lost and directionless, know there is hope. Through the pages of this book, may you find renewed strength and fresh fire in your heart. Though the road may be long and arduous, know your destiny is within reach.

For those who have been battered by the weight of the elephant and are unsure which way to turn, may this book offer comfort and guidance. Despite the chaos and confusion that may surround you, know that trouble cannot stop destiny. With faith and perseverance, you can overcome any obstacle that comes your way. And to those who have lost their way and feel like giving up, know there is a way out. You can pick yourself up and start again with God by your side. May this book give you the strength and grace to confidently move forward, knowing you are not alone. May this book be a source of inspiration and encouragement to all who read it. May it renew your faith and give you the courage to pursue your destiny passionately and purposefully.

Table of Contents

FOREWORD

Written by Natalie Carter UK

I affectionately refer to Vendrix Walker, Delores, Ms. Headley, now Pastor Headley, as my sister, and I mention those names to indicate my comprehensive knowledge of whom I speak. Our close relationship goes way back to our native Island of Jamaica in the small District of Albion Mountain where we grow up together Despite the saying that familiarity breeds contempt, this is not the case with us, as there is always an exception. I share this with you, not to diminish her importance, but to magnify and to include you in her journey of genuineness, authenticity, transparency, experience, and growth.

An evangelist, now ordained pastor, Vendrix Headley is a passionate servant of God. The love to empower, encourage, and counsel drove into several areas on the path to her destiny which was to help many individuals make it to their destination. As inspired by the Holy Spirit, she wrote "When Destiny Calls Trouble Answers." I guarantee you will have a dynamic experience as you flip through the pages of this book.

Prepare for the hush but factual reality of embarking on one's destiny. Vendrix will help you understand that destiny cannot be separated from trouble. This book will help you to be prepared for the unknown on the way to fulfilling your purpose for your future.

The Scripture spoke about the indomitable Mighty Power of God to use the base things of the earth to confound the wisdom of the wise. Here is a living fulfilment of that Scripture by one who has been tested on every element of struggle, rejection, abandonment, and so many other difficulties and is still standing. The fact that you are holding this book in your hand proves that trouble cannot stop destiny. When you are destined for greatness, many troubles will present themselves and God will allow you to go through some hard stuff allowing your faith to be tested so you will learn not to lean on your own understanding but trust Him.

I strongly encourage you to add this exemplary book to your desk and library. You can also take it further by empowering someone you care about and making this book a special gift to them.

ACKNOWLEDGMENTS

I am extremely grateful to Nashon Headley for his invaluable assistance during the brainstorming phase of this book's title. Although he initially expressed hesitation regarding the chosen title, his eventual full comprehension and support were instrumental in bringing the project to fruition. Furthermore, I cherish the moments of shared laughter we experienced during our discussions.

I firmly believe the Holy Spirit played a crucial role in guiding me towards the title and completion of my work, and for this, I am immensely thankful. I am appreciative of the various obstacles and challenges I encountered while writing this book; I literally experienced exactly what the book is all about. They ultimately helped me turn my vision into a concrete reality.

Thanks to Natalie Carter UK for her beautiful foreword.

I would like to express my gratitude to Written Words Publishing LLC for their exceptional work in proofreading and putting the final touches on this book for publication.

INTRODUCTION

When destiny calls, trouble answers. This statement rings true for many of us on the journey to fulfill our purpose in life. It reflects how we feel deep inside when God reveals our destiny through revelation, His spoken word, or dreams, yet our life doesn't reflect the same. Sometimes, it may appear as if our life is heading in a direction that contradicts what we believe God is guiding us towards. We may have a magnificent vision of our future, with God's assurance of fulfilling all our necessities, yet, we might face difficulties like losing a job, defaulting on a mortgage, or facing eviction, among many other things. It is challenging to reconcile the current situation with the vision we have received. However, I have learned that when destiny beckons, hardships often arise.

Destiny cannot be separated from trouble; they go hand in hand. Just as pure gold must go through fire to reach its potential, we must face challenges before fulfilling our destiny. We must make sacrifices and hard decisions on the way to the future God has mapped out for us. The problem is that we often don't acknowledge the relationship between trouble and destiny; we often think we will have a smooth sail, so we are ill-prepared when problems arise. But life is full of twists and turns, and nobody has a smooth sail to their destiny. Along the journey, we are bound to meet bumps and hurdles; through these trials, we are tested and tried. However, not everyone would face the exact weight of troubles.

It is possible that some individuals only encounter minor obstacles and are not tested for an extended period. Despite having everything they desire and living their best life, it may not be evident to the naked eye the effort they put in to maintain that equilibrium. While they may have worked hard to reach their current position, they might have faced minor setbacks or obstacles. Notably, each destiny is different, and what may seem minute to one may be a giant to others; nevertheless, be it minor or large, sacrifices must be made for any significant success to be accomplished.

On the contrary, some individuals endure immense difficulties in reaching their destination. These are the ones who encounter the weight of the elephant. Their path is defined by challenges and hardships which are so burdensome it is remarkable that they have persevered. These individuals may have faced poverty, illness, loss, abandonment, rejection, or discrimination, amongst other trials and had to overcome significant obstacles to survive. Their journey may have been long and arduous, with moments where they felt like giving up. But through it all, they kept pushing forward, determined to reach their destination.

Although two distinct groups of people face different challenges, a shared element unites them. Each group had to surmount obstacles, no matter how daunting or trivial, to reach their present state. While the minor challenges some face may seem insignificant compared to the weight of an elephant, both require fortitude, resilience, and persistence to win. It is important to remember that God will not test us more than we can handle. The troubles and our times of trials are nothing but the preparation for the future God reserved for us. The bigger the problem is, the more significant our breakthrough will be.

This book delves into the inspiring stories of biblical patriarchs who overcame immense challenges to pursue their purpose. Through their experiences, we can learn valuable lessons about facing obstacles with faith. The spiritual aspect of destiny is also explored, highlighting how our beliefs can guide us through difficult times. Each page of this book reveals the relationship between trouble and destiny, emphasizing that destiny can still be achieved despite adversity.

As we journey together through the pages of this book, let us be reminded that our destiny is not a destination but a trip. This journey will require us to endure storms, face our fears, and overcome obstacles. But it is also a journey that will bring us closer to the one who promised us a safe landing, offers us peace amid the storm, and is always with us, even to the end of age.

This book provides inspiration, challenge, and encouragement as we pursue our life's purpose with determination, grace, and appreciation. Keep in mind that when our destiny calls, we will face challenges. However, with steadfast faith, unyielding perseverance, and the unwavering support of God, we can overcome any obstacle and fulfill our life's purpose, leaving behind a legacy that motivates others to follow their paths towards their destiny.

CHAPTER ONE

Destiny and Trouble are Interwoven

"…weeping may endure for a night, but joy cometh in the morning" (Psalm 30:5).

It's not uncommon to ask why things happen the way they do and why we must go through a series of struggles when we believe in the all-knowing and all-powerful God. However, the answer to these questions can be complicated. There are many reasons why we might face difficulties in life. It could be because of our choices, the choices of others, or simply a transformational process that guides us into our destiny. Regardless of the reason, it's essential to understand that these struggles are not in vain. Just as the refining fire is indispensable in purifying gold, so are the trials and challenges we encounter in life essential for our growth and development. These difficulties serve as catalysts, propelling us towards our destined paths and enabling us to attain the highest versions of ourselves. This is something that I've come to understand because I've found myself experiencing breakthroughs right after bad events.

Truly, trouble is how God prepares us for our destiny. In the event that an individual genuinely holds this conviction, how do they approach showing consideration to their difficulty? It's reminiscent of our days as pupils in school when our educators would present us with perplexing brainteasers to work out. At the time, some of us may have questioned the applicability of such activities, yet what was the underlying objective? Participating in puzzle-solving activities has been useful in improving our problem-solving skills, even in unexpected situations where we may need to apply them. Similarly, there are times when we may feel abandoned by God, but it is during these moments when He works on us the most, shaping us into better individuals. He is helping us improve our perseverance, patience, and ability to be better givers and individuals. And He does it all while preparing us for a successful journey to our destiny.

It may not seem right that when destiny calls, trouble answers, but that's the reality of life.

Anytime God chooses us to accomplish anything significant, we encounter trouble before we complete the task, and this happens irrespective of how close we are to God or how faithful we are when it comes to fulfilling the will of God. Job's story in the Bible illustrates how trouble and destiny are intertwined. He lived righteously, followed God's commandments, and obeyed God's will. He was even called "blameless" and "upright." Despite his faithfulness, Job's life was not without challenges and, just like us, he was tempted one too many times, but he stood his ground.

The peculiar story of Job began because Satan saw that he was too committed to God and the things of God, and so Satan wanted to bring him down. Satan believed that Job only served God because he had everything he needed in life, challenging Job's faithfulness that God personally attested for. He suggested that if God took away Job's wealth and blessings, Job would curse God and turn away from Him. God knew that would never happen, so He put Job to the test and allowed Satan to take away everything Job had.

First, the Sabe'ans stole Job's livestock, his servants were slain, and his children died in a windstorm the same day. Despite all this, Job remained faithful to God, saying, *"Naked I came from my mother's womb, And naked I shall return there. The Lord gave, and the Lord has taken away; Blessed be the name of the Lord"* (Job 1:21 NKJV). Job had wholly surrendered himself to the will of God, and that's the same attitude we should have when faced with the troubles of life. We need to realize that God gave us everything we have. We didn't come into this world with anything, yet He provided all our needs.

While Job was still grieving for his family, Satan was busy plotting against him the second time as Job did not curse God when he lost everything. Satan inflicted Job with painful boils from the soles of his feet to the top of his head. Job's wife and friends urged him to curse God and die, but Job refused. He maintained his faith, saying, *"Shall we indeed accept good from God, and shall we not accept adversity?"* (Job 2:10 NKJV) This proves how much destiny and trouble are interwoven. They will always be together.

Can you identify with situations that present themselves one after the other? How do you handle times when one problem has not passed before another comes? Don't be a Christian who believes in God in the good times and then questions His sovereignty as God during rough circumstances. Be like Job instead. Through his suffering, Job learned that genuine, faithful steadfastness means trusting God at all times. He knew God was sovereign and that he had a purpose for every situation in life. Job's faithfulness was rewarded when God restored his wealth and blessed him with new children, double what he had before. The Bible recorded that the latter days of Job were more than his beginning.

Job's story serves as a reminder that challenges and difficulties are an inevitable part of life. Even when we remain faithful, we must continue to trust in God and have unwavering faith that He will guide us through our trials and tribulations. Job's story also reminds us that God has a purpose for our lives, and sometimes, our problems and challenges are meant to strengthen us and prepare us for the great destiny God has in store for us.

If we thought that Job was old enough and that's why he could overcome the troubles and still hold fast to God, then we would be wrong because Joseph also experienced the same at a very young age. Joseph was only 17 when he was sold by his brothers, whose hearts were poisoned by jealousy. Before this time, God shared glimpses of Joseph's destiny with him in dreams, showing that he would be a ruler and a great man. What was Joseph supposed to think when his brothers sold him for 20 pieces of silver and then he was resold in Egypt, where he became enslaved? To worsen the situation, Joseph's tribulations didn't stop there; he was also imprisoned for a crime he did not commit. However, all of Joseph's trials and tribulations were to prepare him for the day he became second in command in Egypt. He would not have been in Egypt if his brothers did not sell him. If he were not enslaved, he wouldn't have been able to enter Pharaoh's palace, and he wouldn't have interpreted Pharaoh's dreams or evaded an audience with the king of Egypt.

Troubles hold the place of molding us into whom God wants us to be. So, whenever we are faced with any troubling situation or circumstance, it's imperative to remember that God, the potter, is at the wheel and we, the clay, have no other option but to trust Him. As believers, we must understand that our trials and troubles do not come based on what we can handle but on what God can handle. Know that He will not let any difficulty come our way that we cannot bear. Joseph thought the first and second trials came with no signs of breakthrough anytime soon. Like Joseph, we have no idea when or where the destiny God is preparing to take us will materialize, which

<u>can be frustrating</u>. We need to trust in the guidance of our God. We must believe that He controls everything and move according to His command. Don't lose heart; as we explore the concept of destiny and the role that trouble plays in our pursuit of it, we find purpose in our struggles.

Staying motivated and pursuing meaningful goals can be challenging when faced with difficulties. It may seem counterintuitive, but the absence of certain conditions can make it even more difficult to feel inspired. After all, when things are going well, shouldn't we feel the most motivated? The opposite is often true. When facing difficulties, we must rise to the occasion and push ourselves to overcome obstacles. This struggle can be a powerful source of motivation, driving us to work harder and make ourselves more fruitful than we ever thought possible. Conversely, when we experience a period of relative ease and comfort, we may become complacent and lose the drive to pursue our goals. We may begin to feel like we have already achieved enough or that we no longer need to put in as much effort as we once did. Without the pressure and urgency of a problematic situation, we may lack the motivation to continue pushing ourselves towards greatness. This is why many people do not pursue their destiny. They are too complacent. However, when God has given us an assignment, He makes sure that He sees us through it, even if it means sending a hurdle our way to get us moving. These hurdles could be anything from financial struggles to health or relationship problems. But the good news is that God never gives us more than we can bear. He knows our limits and will never leave us to face our obstacles alone. When we rely on Him and put our trust in His plan, we can have faith that He will see us through even the most challenging times. Remembering that God's timing is not always ours is essential. We want things to happen immediately, but God knows when the timing is right. Sometimes, we must go through trials and tribulations before we are ready to receive the blessings God has in store for us. Don't shy away from troubles and don't be the person who cowers when things get hard or the person who runs away. We must never forget that God already has a way out of every situation. Whatever trouble we may face in the storm or in the darkness, He is our light. However rough life may be, trust God's ways to see us through.

We must remain prepared and fulfilled to achieve our goals and destinies. We must remember that trouble is often a necessary step in the journey, and we must be ready to face it head-on. By anticipating potential challenges and obstacles, we can prepare ourselves to overcome them, no matter what. This way, we won't be surprised when trouble arrives. Instead, we will already have the tools and mindset necessary to overcome any adversity that comes our way. However, staying prepared and focused does not mean we should stop praying to God for help and guidance. It's okay to ask God to guide us and remove obstacles from our lives. Even Jesus, who came to earth to die for our sins, asked God to take away the cup of suffering that awaited Him. He knew that His destiny was to fulfill God's plan, yet He still asked for help from His Father. We, too, can turn to God for strength and courage to face our challenges.

It's important to remember that just because we pray for help doesn't mean our troubles will magically disappear. Sometimes, God uses our struggles and challenges to help us grow and develop into the person He has destined us to be. It's up to us to trust in God's plan and have faith that He will provide us with the strength and guidance we need to overcome any obstacles that come our way.

My Prayer

Dear God, I ask that you help me embrace the challenges I face in life with the knowledge that it's all part of Your plan to prepare me for my destiny in You. Teach me not to forget that troubles won't last always and that I must overcome them. Please give me the courage to stand steadfast for You and Your will during troubles. Please help me to be committed to my destiny in You and be focused when that destiny is realized. In Jesus' Name, Amen.

My Commitment

Like Job, I will not mock God amid my troubles; I will not curse God. I will hold fast to my faith, knowing that all I have lost will undoubtedly be recovered in ten folds and even if this recovery doesn't unfold before my eyes as soon as I want it, I will keep trusting God—the One who gives and takes.

Like Joseph, my faith in God's promises will be vital. I will never doubt Him because the God I serve is the God who makes rulers of prisoners.

CHAPTER TWO

Dread of the Inevitable

The very mention of the words "pit" and "prison" can evoke fear in anyone's heart. Nobody wants to be confined in such places. However, for many Christians, being in a pit or prison is believed to be a part of God's plan for them.

But hold on! Am I suggesting that many Christians are destined to endure the pit or prison? Absolutely! What about prosperity and good health? What about being a leader instead of a follower? What about the abundance of promises in the Bible and the countless messages in the media that encourage us to claim our blessings, live as God's children, and be highly favored? Even though God grants us amazing promises, the path to achieving them isn't always straightforward. If we knew how it would happen, we would abandon our covenant with Him. The favors are endless, which are also part of God's plan. However, many yearn for the blessings without undergoing the refining, purifying, and molding process that comes with suffering in the pit or prison.

When we reflect on Joseph's story from Genesis 37-48, we cannot ignore his time in the pit and prison. At first, Joseph was immature and self-centered when he received special promises from God through dreams and visions. In his youth, he was innocent and shared the details about his future greatness with his brothers. He lacked the necessary spiritual growth and character to fulfill God's plan. He had to endure challenging experiences like pit and prison to mature and develop the qualities required to fulfill his promise.

The pit God lets us encounter is not meant to ruin us but to help us mature. While in the pit, we understand ourselves better and recognize any anger, bitterness, or unforgiveness in our hearts. We realize the futility of our efforts without God and know He is sovereign and in control. However, many of us stay in the pit for an extended period because we refuse to acknowledge our heart's condition and instead blame the devil. Unfortunately, some of us never mature enough to receive God's promises because of our stubbornness.

In challenging situations, we are presented with

the opportunity to confront our thoughts, feelings, and desires. It's a chance to surrender our will to a higher power and transform it into something beautiful. This process involves refining our character by removing impurities. As we progress, we may face fresh challenges that test our dedication to our beliefs. Are we willing to prioritize our faith over everything else, even if it means sacrificing everything? "Hearts of Fire" by Voice of the Martyrs is a collection of inspiring stories that come to mind. Our ability to resist temptation, even in the most challenging circumstances, indicates our preparedness to face any obstacle that comes our way.

In challenging situations, we are presented with the opportunity to confront our thoughts, feelings, and desires. It's a chance to surrender our will to a higher power and transform it into something beautiful. This process involves refining our character by removing impurities.

In prison, are we willing to serve others and deny ourselves? Think about the jobs (or situations) where some of us feel trapped. Are we willing to give our best even when we think our bosses do not treat us fairly? Do we join in with unbelievers and lambaste those who supervise our work? Do we work as unto the Lord so that others can see Christ in us and desire Him? In prison, God refines our character through working with the unlovely and those who "rub us" the wrong way. He prepares us to deal with all kinds of people, mature through what we suffer, and take up the positions and promises God has for us.

Unfortunately, many believe Christian life is a "cake" walk or an easy street, so they are never prepared to deal with suffering. Therefore, when suffering comes through the pit or prison, many fail to go through the process, become bitter or disillusioned, and give up their faith. Remember that Christian life is not always easy, and we must be prepared to face challenges and suffering. The Scripture tells us this is integral to our Christian walk. *"Yea, and all that will live goldy in Christ Jesus shall suffer persecution"* (2 Timothy 3:12). Romans 8:17 reiterates, *"that we suffer with him, that we may be also glorified together."* But through it all, we can trust that God is working in us and preparing us for the future.

Achieving greatness for God requires courage to face challenges such as imprisonment and agony. Never forget that we are not alone in these difficult times. Trust that God will shape our character and prepare us for a position of power.

My Prayer

Dear Lord, in my most challenging moments, help me to demonstrate the Christlike Spirit in me that will reflect Your light so even my accusers will see You through me. I pray they will be remorseful, make a change in their behavior and come to accept You as their Lord and Savior. In Jesus' Name, Amen.

My Commitment

I am committed to please God in all matters knowing that He will get the glory out of my life, and He is working everything out His way to accomplish His perfect purpose in every given situation. I am committed to endure hardship as a good soldier as I remind myself that all things are working for my good and what the enemy meant for evil, God will turn it around for my good.

CHAPTER THREE

Cast Down, Not Destroyed

It is essential to remember that in our struggles, we are not alone. Even when there's no escape route in sight, it's important not to give up. The Scripture teaches us that a righteous person may fall seven times, but they will also get up seven times (Proverbs 24:16). Even Jesus, the most impeccable man who ever walked and lived on earth, stumbled while carrying His cross, but He never allowed it to hinder Him from fulfilling His purpose.

Always keep in mind that the breakthrough is just around the corner. We should not allow ourselves to remain stuck in a rut. Instead, we must take charge of our lives and arise, even if things seem hopeless. It's essential to understand that there's always hope, and Jesus, the Resurrector, has given us abundance and life. Remember that genuine satisfaction can only be attained through salvation.

To achieve success, it's essential to prioritize what matters. The word ARISE is keen to replenish our minds. It is always in the most hopeless of times when Jesus used it to bring resolution and activate the indomitable power of God. It was used to seek God; His righteousness should be our top priority, as everything else will fall into place. David's Psalm is a testament to God's unfailing faithfulness, where he confidently declares, "yet have I not seen the righteous forsaken, nor his seed begging bread" (Psalm 37:25). Taking time to reflect on our priorities is crucial for our personal growth and honesty with ourselves.

Trusting solely on one's expectations is not enough. Instead, placing trust in God, the Almighty who can achieve the impossible, is critical. It's important to understand that His ways and thoughts are significantly different and superior to ours. By grasping this truth, we can effectively comprehend our present situation and take the necessary steps to move forward. We've all experienced cases where we wanted things done and on schedule. However, this mindset leads to failure in God's eyes. The Bible contains a remarkable factual story recorded in the Book of John that emphasizes this point. The tale tells of

Lazarus, Mary, and Martha, who were very close friends of Jesus.

Lazarus was highly regarded by many for his faithfulness as a dear friend, wise mentor, confidante, and extraordinary healer. Although he held a special place in Jesus' heart, he fell critically ill during Jesus' absence. His sisters implored Jesus to hurry to their aid, convinced that only He had the power to alleviate their beloved brother's suffering. Jesus' arrival was timely and desperately needed, and His capacity to aid was unquestionably relied upon.

Jesus had an excellent plan to bless His friends beyond just healing Lazarus. This caused Him to delay His arrival when called upon, unfortunately resulting in Lazarus' condition worsening and ultimately leading to his death. Mary and Martha were understandably devastated, and their community offered their sympathies. Despite their hope for Jesus' arrival, He did not show up until four days after the burial.

Jesus knew He needed to reveal to His friends that He was much more than they had initially thought. Thus, He intentionally delayed coming to their aid and stayed away from them to bring about the miracle they needed most. Martha was initially disappointed when Jesus didn't show up, but eventually, she ran out to meet Him when He arrived. On the other hand, Mary did not come out to greet Him.

Understandably, Mary felt frustrated with the Master when things didn't go as planned. She expressed her sorrow, saying, "If only you had been here, our brother would still be alive." However, Jesus operates outside of time, as He stated, "A thousand years to us is like a single day to Him." His love and compassion for Lazarus moved Him to tears, and He insisted on being taken to Lazarus' tomb. Despite Martha's doubts that it was too late, as Lazarus had been dead for four days and was already decomposing, with Jesus, there is always hope. We can trust Him to bring a miracle out of our deadly situation. Do you believe it?

With great confidence, Jesus addressed Martha's concerns about her brother's death, reassuring her that He held power to bring him back to life, being the resurrection and the life. Despite the fear of the unpleasant smell, Jesus bravely instructed them to remove the stone that blocked the tomb. After praying to God, He commanded Lazarus to arise from the dead with a powerful voice. All who were present were amazed as Lazarus obeyed and emerged from the tomb, a testament to the incredible power of Jesus.

My dear friends, challenges are an inevitable part of life. However, it is essential not to let them overshadow the blessings that encompass us. Faith must be exercised beyond the natural realm to witness God's miraculous greatness. Unsurprisingly, in difficult times, some individuals lose hope to the point of contemplating taking their own life. We must keep our faith strong, remain hopeful, heed the guidance of the divine, eliminate all barriers, and witness the remarkable might of God in action. Remember that having faith in God empowers us to overcome challenges that may seem insurmountable. The unwavering courage and resilience displayed by Jesus serve as a remarkable model for confronting obstacles with determination. It is reassuring to realize that with divine guidance, we can accomplish far more in a single minute than we could ever manage on our own throughout a lifetime.

My Prayer

Heavenly Father, I look to You for the courage to trust You even when everything seems hopeless. Help me to be confident of Your might and power to do anything even when things get so bad and irredeemable. Help my faith to still stand strong and be unwavering. Father, You are the God of the impossible. Help me to understand that my situation does not take You by surprise and You are not moved by my circumstances but by faith alone. In Jesus' Name, Amen.

My Commitment

I will lift my eyes unto the hills from whence cometh my help. My help comes from the Lord who made Heaven and the earth. I will be obedient to what God's words say. I will not turn to the left nor to the right; I will keep my mind stayed on God. For Him, I live and for Him, I die. I will persevere through my trial trusting God for the victory.

CHAPTER FOUR

Trouble Cannot Stop Destiny

"And not only that, but we also glory in tribulations, knowing that tribulation produces perseverance; and perseverance, character; and character, hope. Now hope does not disappoint, because the love of God has been poured out in our hearts by the Holy Spirit who was given to us" (Romans 5:3-5 NKJV).

The light at the entrance of a tunnel may be noticeable because some natural light can enter. Progressing further into the tunnel, the amount of natural light decreases, and the tunnel becomes darker. This is due to the lack of openings or windows allowing natural light to penetrate. Towards the end of the tunnel, a faint glow of light becomes visible because there may be an opening or exit which also allows some natural light to enter. The light may appear brighter and warmer as near the end of the tunnel, especially if the exit is facing the sun's direction. Overall, the dark tunnel is the darkness that results from the absence of natural light. However, near the end of the tunnel, the presence of natural light helps to illuminate the way and guides toward the destination. We are reminded by the Scripture that the darkest is just before dawn (Mathew 14:25). The phrase, "The darkest hour is just before dawn" was coined by English theologian Thomas Fuller in 1650. This means that even in the bleakest times, there is always hope.

God wants us to understand that no matter how difficult our circumstances may be, they cannot stop us from fulfilling our destiny. Troubles may arise, but they are temporary and will pass. They are like the darkness of the night, which only lasts for a short time before the light of day arrives—just like in the middle of the tunnel. We can be confident that the joy we experience in the morning will far outweigh our troubles at night. This is because the day is longer than the night, and we will have more time to experience joy than we did to have trouble. Therefore, we can be assured that our destiny is secure, and nothing can prevent us from reaching it. We can face our troubles and problems stronger, knowing that they are only temporary and a brighter future lies ahead. Our faith in God and belief in our ability to overcome obstacles will carry us through the darkest times.

But let us not just sing, "Trouble may last for a day, but joy comes in the morning," merely as a song or hymn to provide comfort and hope during difficult times. It's also essential to fully understand their meaning and significance. Instead, we should allow these words to penetrate our hearts and minds and genuinely believe that troubles and hardships are temporary and will eventually end. This belief can help us stay strong and resilient in the face of adversity and allow us to look forward to brighter days.

When I was yet to understand this, I used to think that trouble meant I was going in the wrong direction or maybe I had made a mistake or erred in some way. Sometimes, I would feel like God had abandoned or punished me, and I would ask for forgiveness for my sins instead of strength. I believed that God had set a smooth path and journey for me. But as I gained more spiritual knowledge on trouble and destiny, I started to understand that trouble is part of my journey.

As we grow in Jesus, we realize that trouble is not necessarily a sign that we are on the wrong path. Instead, it is a tool God uses to prepare us for our destiny and, just like any tool, it would be discarded as soon as it has served its purpose. For instance, we might encounter troubles in our lives, and when we talk to God about them, He tells us to trust Him. These troubles are meant to build our faith, and as soon as we surrender to God and start trusting Him for guidance, the trouble will be gone just as fast as it came.

Another instance is when God wants to teach us to be patient and persevere. We may encounter some difficulties with no solution in sight, and when we pray to God, He will give us the "wait" response. The same goes for fear and anxiety. There are moments when I experience a surge of emotions that make me anxious. I tend to overanalyze everything and become uncertain of myself in various aspects. Sometimes, I find myself struggling with negative thoughts and self-sabotage. However, I have found that when I remember to turn to God and cast all my worries upon Him, I immediately feel a sense of relief. So, those who have been experiencing troubles for a long time with no signs of change need to talk to God to gain clarity. They need to understand what the trouble was trying to teach them and show that they have learned the lesson. But before they can do that, they must change their mindset about trouble and understand that trouble may be a bump in the road, but destiny must lead to their destination. They need to realize that for every trial, every tribulation, and every form of trouble, there is a reason to embrace their struggles and learn from them so they can develop a deeper understanding of themselves and their purpose. They must also be prepared to take on their destiny which is right in front of them because their future is so powerful that it cannot be tamed or denied.

Those who have ever felt like they were going through much more trouble than anyone else should know that God is preparing them for something greater than everyone else. We cannot negotiate our destiny or decide to tame it down because of the trouble that comes with a future as big as ours. People like Paul should be our inspiration. Despite being beaten, stoned, shipwrecked, and imprisoned, he never lost faith in God and continued to preach the gospel of Christ. Through his perseverance and unwavering faith, Paul was able to spread the message of Christ to people all over the world. Also, Jonah was ready to be thrown into the sea just so he would not send God's message to the people of Nineveh, but God sent a big fish to swallow him as he was in the water, and the big fish brought him safely to land after three days. In the face of trouble, we must move forward because that's where our destiny is, but this is often easier said than done.

Moving forward in the face of trouble requires both faith and courage. It requires us to trust that God is with us and He has a plan for our lives, even when we cannot see the way ahead. It requires us to take steps of faith, even when the path before us is uncertain. And it needs us to be willing to face our fears and overcome the obstacles that stand in our way. But in all of these, one must remember this: we are not overwhelmed by our strength but by the strength of the power sent to us. As believers in Christ, we are privileged to draw strength from an administration that transcends any obstacle we encounter—the Holy Spirit. This divine force enables us to persist even when our power fails us. Nevertheless, let us learn to rejoice in our suffering like Apostle Paul said in Romans 5:3-5 (NKJV), *"And not only that, but we also glory in tribulations, knowing that tribulation produces perseverance; and perseverance, character; and character, hope. Now hope does not disappoint, because the love of God has been poured out in our hearts by the Holy Spirit who was given to us."* These words are a powerful reminder that our struggles can ultimately cause

31

growth and greater faith. When we face trouble, we can persevere and elope in the character God desires for us. And as we do so, we can trust that our hope in Christ will not disappoint us.

Although trouble cannot impede destiny, it's a mistake to let it distract us from our purpose. This often results in more time dealing with trials and challenges than necessary. We may question how difficulties could divert us from our goal, but it's common to become engrossed in them when encountering trials and tribulations. We may spend countless hours worrying, stressing, and trying to find a way out of our problems. In doing so, we can lose sight of our purpose and the direction we are supposed to be headed in. Trouble can be so distracting that we can end up suspending our destiny. We can become so consumed by our problems that we forget about the bigger picture and the destiny that awaits us. We can also end up doubting ourselves and our abilities and often question whether we can fulfil our purpose or are on the right path. These doubts can further distract us from our goals and cause us to lose focus.

As Christians, we are called to trust in God's plan for our lives and to have faith that He will guide us through any trials and tribulations we may face. It is important to remember that trouble is not an obstacle we cannot overcome but rather a temporary setback that can enlighten us and prepare us for our destiny. Therefore, we must keep trouble from distracting us from our purpose. Instead, we should use it as an opportunity to grow, learn, and fulfil our destiny. By focusing on and resting on God's plan, we can overcome any obstacle that comes our way and fulfil our divine calling.

We must remember that our lives have a purpose and destiny God ordained before birth. However, to reach that destiny, we must rely on the Holy Spirit to guide and strengthen us through all life's troubles. It can be easy to get caught up in our ideas and think that we can accomplish everything on our own, but the truth is that we are limited in our strength. Only through the power of the Holy Spirit can we overcome any obstacle and fulfil our God-given destiny. Just as Jesus fasted and prayed for 40 days and 40 nights to prepare for His ministry, we must also seek God's guidance and strength through prayer and fasting. We must humble ourselves, acknowledge that we cannot do it alone and lean on the Holy Spirit to guide us every step of the way. So, if we find our members are complex, we can turn to the Holy

Spirit for guidance and strength. We should not lose sight of our destiny; we must let the Holy Spirit lead us on the path prepared for us. We can overcome any challenge and fulfil our destiny with faith and trust in God.

My Prayer

Dear God, please help me keep my eyes fixed on You, even in the face of troubles. Help my faith when it is failing and shine in my path when all I see is darkness.

When doubt tries to distract my attention from the destiny You have prepared in front of me, please help me not to be swayed so I may yield to the guidance of the Holy Spirit. Remind me to always turn to You for help whenever I feel stuck in the dark tunnels of trouble. In Jesus' Name, Amen.

My Commitment

Trouble did not stop the destinies of faithful Christ soldiers before me; hardship will not stop my future. I commit to persevere in my Christian journey and always look to Jesus for strength. I will not back down; I will not fold in fear and worry when trouble comes. Instead, I will be bold, knowing that I have the support of the Holy Spirit–my helper.

CHAPTER FIVE

Not By Might Nor Power
But By His Spirit

"...This is the word of the Lord to Zerubbabel: 'Not by might nor by power, but by My Spirit,' Says the Lord of hosts. 'Who are you, O great mountain?...'"
(Zechariah 4:6-7 NKJV).

We can do nothing alone, but all things are possible with Christ who strengthens us through the Holy Spirit. That is the reality that I want us all to walk in. We need to understand and acknowledge the existence of a higher power that can guide and protect us in times of trouble. This higher power is the Spirit of God that resides within us. By placing our trust in this power, we can find the strength and guidance needed to overcome any challenges we may face. Recognizing His power means accepting that we are not alone and there is a force greater than ourselves that can offer support and assistance. By developing a relationship with this power and seeking its guidance, we can navigate through difficult situations and find peace and comfort in knowing that we are being guided by a higher purpose.

The problem is that some of us want to think of logical and practical ways to solve our problems instead of relying on the unexplainable miracles that come with the Spirit of God. Many people believe that God can help them overcome their problems, but sometimes they unknowingly limit that belief. They may have preconceived notions or expectations of how God should solve their problems. However, this can be problematic because it limits God's ability to work in their lives in ways they may not expect or understand. This is often called "putting God in a box." It's as if we're telling the Holy Spirit what and how to do it rather than allowing God's wisdom and guidance to work. When we do this, we rely solely on our own understanding and underestimate what God can do. Believing that God can solve any problem in ways we may not understand is essential. Trusting God means surrendering our preconceptions and letting the Holy Spirit work in us to solve our problems. We may not even realize that we do this, but here's an instance.

When faced with financial challenges, such as paying tuition, we may have prayed to God for help. However, we limit our prayers by asking for a specific solution, such as a job to help earn the money needed to pay the fees. By doing this, we may overlook that God could have other plans for us. We may miss out on opportunities we should have considered because we chose to focus more on a particular outcome. For example, while we may think getting a job is the only way to pay tuition, God may have already prepared a scholarship opportunity. We could have missed this opportunity because we did not leave room for God's plans to unfold. This is an example of why we must avoid limiting God to what we think is possible.

We should be open to the idea that God can provide for us in ways we may never imagine. Instead of asking for a specific solution, we should trust that God has our best interests and He will provide the best possible outcome. We already know that God works in mysterious ways, so why not let Him do what He knows to do best while we do our part?

God meant every word when He said, "Not by might nor by power, but by My Spirit" (Zechariah 4:6). This verse emphasizes that human strength and ability are insufficient to accomplish God's purposes. Still, we can achieve them only by the power of His Spirit. We see this truth exemplified in the life of Gideon in the Book of Judges.

When God called Gideon to lead the Israelites against the Midianites, Gideon doubted his ability. But God assured him, "I will be with you, and you shall defeat the Midianites as one man" (Judges 6:16). Instead of relying on his might or power, Gideon obeyed God and assembled an army of 32,000 men. But God had other plans, and He instructed Gideon to reduce the army to 300 men. With this small group of soldiers, God gave Gideon a miraculous victory over the Midianites, demonstrating that it was not by might nor by power but by God's Spirit that they could triumph.

Ultimately, it is only through the power of the Holy Spirit that we can do anything of eternal value. As Jesus said, "Without Me, you can do nothing" (John 15:5). When we acknowledge our weakness and surrender our lives to God, we can experience the fullness of His strength and power working in us to accomplish His will.

We need to let the Spirit of God be the wind in our sails and not be a passenger on our ship who listens to us and offers advice occasionally. The Holy Spirit can be there all day, all week, and all month, speaking to and guiding us. We must understand that the Holy Spirit is an essential and powerful force that can help us navigate life's challenges. Jesus promised the disciples that He would send the Holy Spirit to guide them. In John 14:26 (NKJV), Jesus said, *"But the Helper, the Holy Spirit, whom the Father will send in My name, He will teach you all things, and bring to your remembrance all things that I said to you."* This promise emphasizes that the Holy Spirit is not just an advisor but a teacher who can lead us in the right direction, and this promise is passed down to us as believers and as those led by the Spirit whom the Apostle Paul calls Sons of God. By yielding to the leading of the Holy Spirit, we become sons of God and heirs of the kingdom.

In addition to being our guide, the Holy Spirit is our comforter. In John 14:16-17 (NKJV), Jesus promised to send the Holy Spirit as a helper, saying, *"And I will pray the Father, and He will give you another Helper, that He may abide with you forever—the Spirit of truth, whom the world cannot receive, because it neither sees Him nor knows Him; but you know Him, for He dwells with you and will be in you."* This passage reveals that the Holy Spirit is not just an external force but an internal one that dwells within us, giving us comfort and guidance, which is all we need when life throws a million curve balls at us.

However, we need to understand that the Holy Spirit is not a crutch for the weak but a source of power that can help us achieve great things. In Acts 1:8 (NKJV), Jesus tells His disciples, *"But you shall receive power when the Holy Spirit has come upon you; and you shall be witnesses to Me in Jerusalem, and in all Judea and Samaria, and to the end of the earth."* Here, Jesus promises that the Holy Spirit will give them the power to be His witnesses to the end of the earth. The disciples were not weak or helpless, but they needed the power of the Holy Spirit to accomplish the task that Jesus had given them.

We also see the story of Samson, a mighty warrior for Israel. He had incredible physical strength, but ultimately, his faith in God gave him power. In Judges 14:6, we read that "the Spirit of the Lord came mightily upon him," allowing him to defeat a lion with his bare hands. Later, when the Philistines captured him, he prayed to God for strength, and the Spirit came upon him again, enabling him to break free and defeat his enemies.

Another example of the power of the Holy Spirit can be found in the story of David and Goliath. When David faced the giant, he did not rely on his strength or skill. Instead, he trusted in the power of God. In 1 Samuel 17:45, David declares, "You come to me with a sword, with a spear, and with a javelin. But I come to you in the name of the Lord of hosts, the God of the armies of Israel, whom you have defied." It was the power of God that enabled David to defeat Goliath, not his abilities. If we want to see a fundamental change in our lives and reach our destiny safely, we must surrender ourselves and rely only on the power of God.

To fully surrender ourselves to God, we must relinquish our desires and trust in His plan. We must recognize that we are not in control and that God's ways are higher than ours. As Jesus said to His disciples in Matthew 16:24-25 (NKJV), *"If anyone desires to come after Me, let him deny himself, and take up his cross, and follow Me. For whoever desires to save his life will lose it, but whoever loses his life for My sake will find it."*

We must be like Abraham who was ready to sacrifice his only son without hesitation. It's not that Abraham didn't love his son; he did, but he was prepared to give him up to please God. Abraham understood that it was God who gives and God who takes. He believed that if God had given him a son before, God could give him another son. That is the kind of faith we should have when we want to rely on the might of the

Holy Spirit. God will not constantly ask us to do easy things like donate to charity or host a food drive to hand out food to the homeless. Some sacrifices that would be required of us will be impossible to be bought with money, just like Abraham. In this time, too, we must trust God and trust that He will be with us from now until the very end of the age.

My Prayer

Dear God, thank You for sending Your Holy Spirit to help me on my journey to destiny. I am grateful that I do not have to navigate through the troubles of life alone and that I have a helper and a friend who is always with me. In Jesus' Name, Amen.

My Commitment

I will no longer tell God how to save me from troubles. Instead, I will let Him have His way and do His will. I affirm that my human strengths are insufficient, and so I commit to not relying on my strength and relying solely on God.

I surrender the driver's seat of my life to You, God, and let You lead me through the paths You have designed for me. I let go of my fleshy desires for control and yield entirely to Your guidance.

CHAPTER SIX

Visualize the Vision

"Where there is no vision, the people perish..."
(Proverbs 29:18).

As believers, we are encouraged to rely on faith instead of sight. Nonetheless, we can still harness the strength of visualization to conquer our challenges and fulfil the purpose God has bestowed upon us. Having a clear visualization of the vision that God has instilled in our hearts can be a potent tool in keeping us motivated, focused, and confident in facing challenges. It also helps us chart a course towards achieving our goals.

The story behind the great fall of Jericho is the perfect example of the power of visualization. After Moses died, God appointed Joshua as the new leader of the Israelites. He commanded Joshua to lead them into the Promised Land, a journey that Moses had started. One of the first obstacles Joshua and his army faced was the fortified city of Jericho. The town was heavily guarded and the walls were so thick that it seemed impossible for the Israelites to penetrate them. However, God had given Joshua a vision of victory, and he instructed the Israelites to march around the city once a day for six days, with seven priests blowing trumpets made of ram's horns. On the seventh day, they were to march around the city seven times, and when they heard the long blast of the trumpet, all the people were to shout and the walls of Jericho would fall. Despite the apparent foolishness of this plan, Joshua obeyed God's command and the Israelites marched around the city as instructed. When the people shouted, the walls of Jericho fell and the Israelites were able to take the city. The story of Joshua showcases the strength of faith and visualization in fulfilling God's plans. Despite facing a seemingly insurmountable task, Joshua remained steadfast in his trust in God's vision and dutifully followed His guidance. Joshua was focused, motivated, and confident during adversity by visualizing the promised victory and the image of the falling wall.

We can harness the benefits of visualization and faith to conquer challenges and fulfil the goals instilled in us by God. By concentrating on His promises and picturing the result He has designed for us, we can maintain our drive and self-assurance, even in seemingly insurmountable circumstances. The visualization practice remains relevant today, regardless of whether one has received God's divine vision of their life. What truly matters is that the teachings of the Bible hold a significant place in one's life. Its promises apply to the believers and provide them with a vision to imagine. It can be a dream where God's thoughts for us will be brought to fruition or a picture where there will be no sick one amongst us. This vision inspires action in our lives. We can't just sit around and hope that God's promises to us will come to life. We must put in the work, but we cannot make frivolous decisions. We have to follow God's Word.

Every promise that God makes comes with a commandment that we need to obey or criteria we need to meet before the blessings from the promise contract work in our life. For example, God says that all things would work together for our good, and we repeat this in different variations, but the central idea is the same; if we love God, everything will work for good in our life. God also promised us that we would live a long life if we honored our parents and that He would forgive us if we forgive others who have wronged us.

So why does God attach a commandment to His promises? I believe it's because obedience is essential to our relationship with God. By following His commandments, we demonstrate our trust in Him and willingness to submit to His authority. Obedience also helps us align our lives with God's purpose and plan, leading to greater joy and fulfilment. For example, if we believe that God has promised to bless us financially, we should also be mindful of the commandment to be good stewards of our resources and to give generously to others. Or if we believe that God has promised to provide us with a fulfilling career, we should also be aware of the commandment to work with integrity and to use our talents to serve others. We can create a roadmap for our lives rooted in His will and purpose by aligning our vision with God's promises and commandments. This approach can help us avoid pursuing goals and desires that are ultimately unfulfilling or harmful and instead focus on what truly matters in our relationship with God and our service to others.

When our vision is aligned with the will of God, we are no longer limited by our human abilities or resources. Instead, we are empowered by the Holy Spirit and able to accomplish great things. As the Apostle Paul wrote in Philippians 4:13, we can do all things through Christ who strengthens us. When we trust in God and seek His will for our lives, we can overcome any obstacle and achieve our goals. However, it's important to note that aligning our vision with God's will requires surrendering ourselves and plans. Proverbs 3:5-6 instructs us to trust in the Lord with all our heart and lean not on our own understanding; in all our ways submit to Him, and He will direct our paths. When we submit to God and trust His plan, we can experience His blessings and grace.

Visualizing our vision is so crucial in the race to destiny. It is the first step towards creating the reality we want to experience. It's not just wishful thinking; it is intentionally seeing ourselves where we want to be and planning how to get there. Visualization lets us know exactly what we need to actualize our vision, making attracting the resources we need in faith much easier.

The Bible tells us, *"Where there is no vision, the people perish…"* (Proverbs 29:18). We must always keep our vision and trust God's plan. When we visualize our concept, we can better focus our thoughts and energies towards achieving our goals. We can also see the bigger picture and understand that our challenges are temporary setbacks on our journey towards our destiny. In other words, where there is vision, the people prosper. Also, the more precise our vision is, the higher our chances are of staying on the course of our destiny. Our ideas are like a map that guides us to our future, without which we could easily get lost.

We don't talk much about Nehemiah, but his faith and vision inspired others to join him in the work, and together they rebuilt the walls and restored Jerusalem to its former glory. Nehemiah was a man of faith with a strong vision for the restoration of Jerusalem. This vision was so evident in his mind that he could almost see it. Nehemiah's ability to visualize his dream was the key to his success. He could paint a clear picture of what he wanted to achieve, which gave him the focus and determination to see it through. He knew that rebuilding the walls of Jerusalem would be a monumental task, but he believed that it could be done. Nehemiah's faith in God was also a driving force behind his vision. He thought that God had called him to lead this project and that He would provide the resources and support needed to make it a reality. This faith gave Nehemiah the courage to take on this enormous task and to persevere even in the face of significant opposition.

Despite facing many obstacles, Nehemiah never lost sight of his vision. He remained focused on rebuilding Jerusalem's walls and restoring the city to its former glory. He rallied others to join him in this mission and together they completed the work. Nehemiah's faith and vision paid off. He led the successful rebuilding of the walls of Jerusalem, and the city was restored to its former greatness. His ability to visualize his vision and his unwavering faith in God were the key factors that led him to reach his destiny.

Nehemiah's story serves as an inspiration to us all. It reminds us of the power of visualization and faith in achieving our goals. By showing a clear picture of what we want to achieve and trusting in God to guide us, we can also reach our destinies and make a difference in the world. But what steps are we taking right now? Do we even know the vision that God has for our life? We need to go back to God and seek His face, asking for Him to open our eyes to understanding so we can see where He plans to take us. Nothing is easy about waiting for our vision and pursuing our dream in God.

My Prayer

Dear Lord, please open my eyes to see the vision of my life and give me the grace to walk in that vision. Please obey any commandment that is tied to the realization of Your vision for my life. When I finally get to walk in the reality that You have designed for me, please give me the grace to remain steadfast in obeying Your will. In Jesus' Name, Amen.

My Commitment

I will always walk by faith and not sight. I will be focused, motivated, and confident in God's power to see me through life's troubles.

I will not see impossibilities; I will only see possibilities because I trust in a God who has the power to make all things possible.

I choose faith over fear. I prefer the vision God has shown me through His Word and prophecies over the lies that the devil whispers in my ear.

CHAPTER SEVEN

Crucified Flesh for Your Journey

"I have been crucified with Christ; it is no longer I who live, but Christ lives in me; and the life which I now live in the flesh I live by faith in the Son of God, who loved me and gave Himself for me" (Galatians 2:20 NKJV).

If there's anyone who has faced the most trouble on their journey to destiny, then it would be Jesus Christ. Right from the moment He was born in a humble manger to the day He was crucified on the cross, He was sought after to be killed. Yet, Jesus remained steadfast in His destiny to redeem us from sin and death. As the Son of God, Jesus left Heaven to come to a world filled with sinners. He came not to be served but to help and give us His life as a ransom. He knew the purpose of His existence, and He was willing to pay the ultimate price for it. Jesus' journey to His destiny was marked by selflessness, compassion, and a deep love for humanity.

Jesus' ministry on earth was one of love and service to others. He healed the sick, fed the hungry, and cared for the poor. He was always on the move, reaching out to lost and forgotten people. He had a heart for the poor and weak, and His teachings were centered on love, forgiveness, and grace. These three traits would make the world better if everyone had one. However, despite all He did for us, we still turned on Him. The same people He was trying to save were trying to kill Him. He was rejected by His people, the Jewish leaders, and the Roman authorities accused Him, beat Him, and eventually, crucified Him on the cross. His death was a painful and humiliating experience, but it was also a necessary sacrifice for the salvation of humanity.

The Bible records no greater love than that Jesus displayed on the cross. He willingly gave up His life for the sake of others, even those who hated Him. He forgave His executioners and He prayed for their salvation. His death was the ultimate sacrifice; one that would bring salvation and eternal life to all who believe His life was a testament to His love for humanity, and His death was the ultimate expression of that love. Through His death and resurrection, we can reach our destinies in Him. Jesus has set the tone for us and shown us how to achieve if we are selfless and show compassion for one another.

The call to follow Jesus is not easy, and honestly, many would not because of the responsibility and the sacrifices required. We must die before we can live with Him. But this death is necessary as it is through it that we find true life in Christ. Paul explains it properly in Romans 6:6-7, *"Knowing this, that our old man is crucified with him, that the body of sin might be destroyed, that henceforth we should not serve sin. For he that is dead is freed from sin."* Here, Paul also reminds the church that our old selves and sinful nature have been crucified with Christ when we accept Christ. This means we are no longer slaves to sin and we have the power to resist temptation and live according to God's will. This is Christ's reality and the gift He gave us when we chose Him.

Noting this, Paul said, *"I have been crucified with Christ; it is no longer I who live, but Christ lives in me; and the life which I now live in the flesh I live by faith in the Son of God, who loved me and gave Himself for me"* (Galatians 2:20 NKJV). He emphasized that the life we live as believers is not our own but Christ living in us. Our old selves have been crucified with Christ, and we now live by faith in Him.

Jesus also speaks about the call to die to oneself

in Luke 9:23-24 (NKJV), *"If anyone desires to come after Me, let him deny himself, and take up his cross daily, and follow Me. For whoever desires to save his life will lose it, but whoever loses his life for My sake will save it."* Here, Jesus calls us to deny ourselves and our desires and follow Him. He tells us that those willing to die for Him will find eternal life.

Death to self and life in Christ is the only way to overcome troubles and reach our destiny. This is an age-old truth that has been preached since the beginning of Christianity. To truly live the life God has called us to, we must die to ourselves and allow Christ to live in us. It means letting go of our desires and ambitions and surrendering to God's will. Through this death to self, we find true life and freedom. When we offer our will to God's will, we can experience a peace that surpasses all understanding. The cares of this world no longer weigh us down; instead, we can rest in the knowledge that God is in control.

This death to self doesn't just happen once. It's not a decision we make today that just sticks. Death to self is a daily choice that we must push through intentional submission to the will and doctrines of God alone. We must constantly examine our lifestyle and actions and seek God's will. In this death, Christ gives us life—a life that is rooted in faith, hope, and love. He transforms us from the inside out, and we become more like Him daily. This is not always easy, as we are constantly bombarded with distractions and temptations that can lead us astray. However, if we are committed to living by God's plan, we must consciously seek His will and follow His lead.

So, where do we go from here? How do we figure out what God's will is for our lives? The answer can be found in the final command that Jesus gave to His disciples before He ascended into Heaven. He said, "Go ye into all the world, and preach the gospel to every creature" (Mark 16:15). This is God's will for us, and only when we align ourselves with this will we know we are walking in His destiny.

It is important to note that this does not mean we must all become pastors or missionaries. God can use anyone from any profession or walk of life to fulfil His purposes. Joseph, the earthly father of Jesus, was a carpenter, and David was a shepherd boy before he became a king. God is not interested in our qualifications or our social status. While on earth, He clearly said that He came for the sinners. He is interested in our hearts and our willingness to obey His commands. When we surrender to God's will, He will equip us with the necessary tools and resources to guide us to our destiny and help us fulfil His purposes. He doesn't call the qualified; instead, He qualifies those He calls. Like clay, He wants to mold us to fit His plans for our lives; like gold, He wants to refine us and remove our impurities. If we are willing to step out in faith and trust in His provision, then we can be assured that He will guide us and empower us to do His will.

My Prayer

Dear God, please give me the courage to lay down my flesh for my journey to destiny. Help me to be consistent even when I'm not appreciated or applauded, and if I'm approved, help me not to be influenced by the pride of being placed on a pedestal. Help me to be like Jesus, who, though He was and is the Son of God, chose to serve rather than be served during His lifetime on earth. Teach me what it means to be humble and help me live according to Your teachings. Teach me to die to myself so I can live with You. In Jesus' Name, Amen.

My Commitment

Like Paul, I am crucified with Christ and commit to living a life that exemplifies this crucifixion. I let go of my desires and am fully committed to the will of God. The world's cares will not weigh me down because I am not of the world. By the power of God, I overcome every temptation that comes my way.

CHAPTER EIGHT

Your Cross Is Your
Ticket into Heaven

"Then said Jesus unto his disciples, If any man will come after me, let him deny himself, and take up his cross, and follow me" (Matthew 16:24).

The cross is a symbol of faith in Christendom, and it also represents our belief in Jesus Christ and the suffering that He endured on the cross for all our sakes. While appreciating Jesus' sacrifice on the cross and how selfless He was, we must also keep in mind that the purpose of His sacrifice was for our salvation. It was not to show that He was the Son of God or that He could die and rise again. Jesus died for us to be free from sin so that the name of God will be glorified in our life. In His death, He gave salvation free of charge for anyone willing to come after Him, deny himself, and take up his cross.

Receiving salvation, therefore, means that we

must leave it all. We must leave everything we think we have including ourselves and follow Jesus. And if we truly genuinely want to follow Jesus, we must go the way He went. We must also face the challenges and the hardships that He met and eventually endure until the end, just like He did, demonstrating our commitment to living a life that reflects the values and teachings of Jesus Christ.

In our obedience to Jesus and our commitment to following Him, we would find our cross, our ticket into God's kingdom. Our cross represents the hardship that we will face on our journey. It means our responsibility to spread the gospel and preach the word of life to all nations. So that in the end, we will be welcomed with open arms into Heaven, where we will be called faithful.

Our life on earth should have more to do with what God wants and less with what we want. We must recognize in the first place that it is God who placed us here and we are here to do His work, not ours. In Matthew 16, while admonishing His disciples, Jesus asked them, "Whom do you say that I am?" This question was crucial in the disciples' relationship with Jesus, as it forced them to confront their beliefs about His identity and mission. Peter answered, "You are the Christ, the

Son of the living God," and Jesus replied, "Blessed are you, Simon, son of Jonah, for this was not revealed to you by flesh and blood but by my Father in Heaven." This exchange affirmed Peter's faith and established him as a leader among the disciples.

This moment in Matthew 16 also marks a turning point in Jesus' ministry as He prepared His disciples for His upcoming death and resurrection. He told them that He must go to Jerusalem and suffer many things at the hands of the elders, chief priests, and law teachers and that He would be killed and raised to life on the third day. Still basking in the glow of His confession, Peter rebuked Jesus for talking about such things, but Jesus sharply rebuked him in return, saying, "Get behind me, Satan!" This exchange between Jesus and Peter illustrates the tension between the disciples' earthly desires and God's higher purposes. Peter, like many of the Jews of his time, was expecting the Messiah to be an influential political leader who would overthrow the Roman occupation and establish a Jewish kingdom. Jesus, however, had a different mission: to save humanity from sin and reconcile them to God. This required Him to suffer and die, and Peter's rebuke was a temptation to take an easier path.

Jesus noticed that they were still struggling to understand the true nature of His mission on earth. He then turned to them and said, "If anyone would come after me, let him deny himself and take up his cross and follow me." These words of Jesus have been echoed throughout the centuries and have become a cornerstone of Christian theology. But what exactly does it mean to take up your cross and follow Jesus?

Firstly, it means denying oneself. We must be willing to put aside our wants, dreams, and personal goals to serve God and others. This act requires a deep level of selflessness and sacrifice. By carrying our cross, we must be willing to acknowledge that our life is not the most essential thing in the world. We are not the center of the universe, and our interests and ambitions should not take priority over the needs of others. Instead, our life should be focused on serving a greater purpose—following God's commandments and using our gifts and skills to impact the lives of people around us positively. Essentially, we are required to prioritize the needs of others over our own desires.

Nowadays, many Christians focus on being receivers rather than givers. We often find ourselves consumed by the idea of receiving more and more. We focus on acquiring wealth, status, and possessions and constantly crave more. Unfortunately, this mindset has also seeped into our spiritual lives, and we have become more focused on what God can give us rather than what we can give to God and others. Our prayers are often centered around asking God to provide us with what we want instead of asking God what He wants us to do for others. We tend to approach prayer as if placing an order for our needs rather than seeking God's will for our lives.

The Bible teaches us that we are called to be givers, just as God is a giver. John 3:16 says, *"For God so loved the world, that he gave him only begotten Son, that whosoever believeth in him should not perish, but have everlasting life."* God gave His only Son as a sacrifice for our sins so that we could have eternal life. This is the ultimate example of giving, and we are called to follow in God's footsteps. Giving is a significant part of taking up our cross as Christians. We should be willing to give sacrificially to others, just as God gave to us. We can provide our time, talents, and resources to help those in need. We can show kindness, compassion, and love to those hurt or under challenging situations. Doing so reflects God's love for the world and fulfils His purpose for our lives. We should also focus on giving back to God. This means we should give Him our time, attention, and devotion. We should pray, worship, study the Bible, and obey His commandments. When we give our lives to God, we experience true fulfilment and joy.

In the time of Jesus, the cross symbolized shame, suffering, and death, which hasn't changed much. Even if no one puts us on the cross to crucify us, we will still face significant challenges just because we chose to follow Jesus. By taking up our cross, we acknowledge that following Jesus may not be easy. We may face persecution, rejection, and hardship. But we are called to endure these trials and tribulations with faith, knowing that God is with us every step of the way.

Finally, taking up the cross means following Jesus. We are called to imitate His life and teachings, to be His disciples in every sense of the word. This means living a life of love, service, and sacrifice. It means putting the needs of others before our own, just as Jesus did.

As Christians, we are not called to live comfortable and effortless lives. We are called to take up our cross and follow Jesus, no matter where that road may lead us. Remember when God called Abraham when he was still Abram to leave his kindred journey to a new land he did not know about. God said, "Go forth from your country, your kindred, and your father's house to the land I will show you." That was all Abraham needed to hear. He didn't doubt or question the voice of God; he just went, trusting God wholly. Confused and scared, he knew he had to take up his cross and follow Jesus. Leaving everything behind, he took his wife, Sara, and nephew, Lot, and embarked on a journey that would change his life forever.

Abraham's story is a powerful example of what it means to have faith in God and to follow His call, even when it leads us into the unknown. It is a reminder that, as Christians, we are called to step out of our comfort zones and trust in God's plan for our lives, even if that means leaving behind everything we know and love.

This call to take up our cross and follow Jesus echoes throughout the New Testament. This is a challenging task. It requires sacrifice, self-denial, and a willingness to surrender our desires and plans to follow God's will for our lives. But the rewards of following Jesus far outweigh the costs. Through our obedience and faith, we can experience a deep and meaningful relationship with God, receive His blessings, and positively impact the world. Of course, following Jesus doesn't always mean leaving everything behind and embarking on a physical journey as Abraham did. Sometimes, it simply means obeying God's call in our daily lives, even if that means making small sacrifices or stepping out of our comfort zones. It might mean forgiving someone who has hurt us deeply, even when we don't feel like it. It might mean speaking up for what is right, even when it's unpopular. Or it might mean choosing to love and serve others, even when inconvenient or uncomfortable.

Whatever form it takes, the call to take up our cross and follow Jesus is a call to live a life of purpose and meaning. It is a call to trust in God's plan for our lives and to follow wherever He leads us. And in doing so, we can experience the fullness of life that God has in store for us.

But we need help to walk this road. We have the Holy Spirit to guide us and each other to encourage and support us. We must exercise faith and rely entirely on Him for guidance and direction. Only then can we hear His voice and follow His lead.

My Prayer

Dear God, please help me to avoid getting to the gift of the cross. Quicken my Spirit so that I remain in awe of Your sacrifice and never lose sight of the purpose of that sacrifice, which is to grant salvation, free for all. Let the cross be my compass in my journey to destiny, guiding me toward truth and Your kingdom. In Jesus' Name, Amen.

My Commitment

I deny myself and take on the cross, following in the paths Jesus had walked while He was on earth. In my Christian journey, I commit to living a life of selflessness and sacrifice, just as Jesus did. I commit to continuously deepening my understanding of His teachings and applying them daily.

CHAPTER NINE

The Footman

"If you have run with the footmen, and they have wearied you, Then how can you contend with horses? And if in the land of peace, In which you trusted, they wearied you, Then how will you do in the floodplain of the Jordan?"
(Jeremiah 12:5 NKJV).

The footman represents the small challenges we face on the journey to fulfilling our destiny in Christ. The obstacles might seem insignificant, but they signify spiritual growth and development. The footman in our spiritual growth can be anything from a minor temptation that tests our resolve to a small act of kindness that helps us practice compassion and empathy towards others. It's important to remember that even the most minor challenges can impact our character and ultimately shape our spiritual journey. So we must not underestimate the value of the footman in our life, and we should use each challenge to strengthen our faith and become a better version of ourselves.

I remember a time when I faced one of these footmen. I was going through a rough patch financially; I was late on my bills and had no hope of where the money would come from. I trusted that God would make a way; I needed a miracle, but did I get one? One month, I received a notice that my shop's $8,000 electricity bill was overdue and I had to pay promptly to prevent disconnection. Unfortunately, I did not have sufficient funds. This left me feeling quite helpless and frustrated. Despite my best efforts, I could not arrange the required funds before the due date passed. I tried to get extra time to pay, but I couldn't. However, I was asked to pay about $1,275 to stop the disconnection for that moment and then start a new plan for paying off my bill. But I still couldn't make the payment because I was present at the shop and the electric company couldn't wait for me, so they cut it off. Thankfully, my sons were able to settle and get the service reconnected.

At first, I was angry and upset that I couldn't do anything to help the situation. I felt like I was being punished for something out of my control. But as the hours went by, I began to see things differently. I realized this was just one of the footmen on my journey, and I needed to overcome it if I wanted to move forward. Looking back, I can see how this experience helped me to grow and develop as a person. It taught me the importance of perseverance and resilience and strengthened my faith in God. May I add that the following month a miracle happened. When I looked at my statement, $5,000 was subtracted from my account. Lord, I don't need to understand; all I need is to hold Your hand.

Like how children grow up, we will grow in our faith in Christ. However, God will not give us significant responsibilities right away. Instead, He will provide us with more minor faults and gradually increase them. We are assimilable to handle these more minor responsibilities before we can take on the bigger ones. These small tasks help us develop essential skills and qualities such as diligence, faithfulness, and trustworthiness. So, let's not be discouraged by the small jobs we are given. Instead, let's embrace and do them to the best of our abilities. As we do this, God will see that we are faithful in the small things and will eventually trust us with more significant things.

Remember, just like how a child grows and learns step by step; we must grow in our faith and trust in Christ step by step. This is one of the beauties of young Christianity—not understanding that everything happens according to God's timing and season. I call it a beauty because of the passion and the zeal with which Christians ask God for grandiose powers, such as raising the dead, and then they get angry and confused when they can't heal the sick. I went through this stage, too, much like any other Christian, with a million questions. I had "why(s)" and "when(s)" that needed to be answered, but no one was giving me the answers I desperately desired.

However, as I grew in my faith, I understood that God's power works in different ways, and it may not always align with what we think we need or want. Through my journey as a Christian, I understood that sometimes God's plan differs from ours. He may choose to heal someone differently or not at all, and it's essential to trust in His wisdom and love, even when we don't understand. While it's natural to desire big things and miraculous powers, it's important to remember that God's power works in different ways and often in ways we may not expect. It's essential to continue to pray for the things we need and want and to trust in God's plan and timing, even when it doesn't match our own.

I then learned something important about growing in faith. I realized that every time we want to become more powerful in Christ, we must face a challenge. This challenge is like a footman who guards the way to our goal. It would be best to overcome this challenge to reach the power we want in our faith. In other words, we must work hard to overcome obstacles before achieving our goals. It's like climbing a mountain. We need to climb the first few steps to reach the top. Similarly, if we don't overcome the obstacles in our path, we won't be able to access the power of Christ we desire.

As a loving father, it is God's wish that we succeed, progress and eventually reach the destiny that He has designed for us, but still, He won't put us in situations we are unprepared for. Think of it like a game, where each level presents new challenges that we need to overcome to progress to the next level. In the same way, God won't allow us to face challenges we are not yet equipped to handle. He won't put us before a footman until we are ready to fight and overcome it. This is because He knows we need to gain experience and knowledge to conquer the challenge truly. So, when we face small challenges, we must see them as opportunities to grow and learn. We should take the time to prepare ourselves and gain the necessary skills to overcome these challenges. With God's help and guidance, we can move on to the next level of our lives and face more enormous difficulties with confidence and strength.

Apart from external challenges and obstacles, the footman symbolizes personal habits we must overcome before God can give us more significant responsibilities. We may face challenges that require changing our practices to become better individuals. These habits, such as procrastination, laziness, or negative thinking, can prevent us from reaching our full potential. In the same way, when we want to serve God, we must first address these personal habits that hinder us from being effective servants. We need to be disciplined, responsible, and accountable for our actions. Only then can we be entrusted with greater responsibilities and significantly impact the world. The good thing is that God will not cast us out because we still struggle with these habits. Instead, He will help us overcome the habits and addictions so we can become a better person who is more like Him.

Look at Gideon. He was hesitant, insecure, and filled with doubt, yet God still chose him. God helped Gideon overcome his fears through tests and trials and become a mighty leader. In Judges 6:12-16, an angel of the Lord appeared to Gideon and said, "The Lord is with you, mighty warrior." Gideon questioned his strength by asking, "How can I save Israel? My clan is the weakest in Manasseh, and I am the least in my family." But God reassured Gideon, saying, "I will be with you, and you will strike down all the Midianites, leaving none alive." God then gave Gideon a series of signs to confirm his calling, and Gideon began to trust in God's plan for him. However, Gideon still had doubts and fears. In Judges 7:2-7, God instructed Gideon to reduce his army from 32,000 to 300 men. Although this seemed impossible, Gideon obeyed and God delivered an excellent victory for Israel against their enemies.

Through this story, we see how God can use even those who doubt themselves and struggle with personal habits to accomplish great things. We can become mighty warriors in improving our service by prioritizing our purpose, resisting our fleshly desires, and trusting God to help us overcome our weaknesses.

God expects us to surpass challenges without exhaustion before He assigns other tasks, but we should remember that we are not solely responsible for accomplishing this alone.

Remember, we can do everything through Christ who strengthens us. He would prepare us for the job ahead just as He prepared that lamb for sacrifice in place of Isaac, Abraham's only son. God will ensure we are ready to face our challenges head-on, and He will personally prepare us for the battle, so why do we worry?

The Bible reassures us that God will always be with us, and He won't just be a silent observer; He will actively support us. In Isaiah 41:10 (NKJV), God said, *"So do not fear, for I am with you; do not be dismayed, for I am your God. I will strengthen and help you; I will uphold you with my righteous right hand."* Regardless of our challenges, we should rest assured because we know that God will strengthen us. In 1 Corinthians 10:13 (NKJV), He cautions us not to be weary and throws us into overthinking by saying, *"No temptation has overtaken you except such as is common to man; but God is faithful, who will not allow you to be tempted beyond what you are able, but with temptation will also make the way of escape, that you may be able to bear it."* This convinces us that God will never give us more than we can handle and will provide a way to endure our challenges. Don't worry about the challenges ahead; God will prepare us for them.

However, I must acknowledge that it's easy for

me to say don't worry about the challenges ahead, but it's much harder not to worry about them. It's natural to feel worried and anxious. Sadly, that's a die-hard trait of the flesh. Sometimes, we worry about the future, sometimes about the present, and sometimes we fear without knowing the reason because we have a loving God who knows the end from the beginning and has assured us that all things will work for our good because we love Him. He has seen our future and knows it is good, so why should we worry? Why should we doubt him? We shouldn't.

My Prayer

Dear God, please help me to grow even more dependent on You. Help me turn to You when I face challenges—big or small. When I'm in doubt, strengthen my faith in Your ability to pull me through and remind me of Your power and love. Fill my heart with an unwavering belief, knowing that anything is possible with You. In Jesus' Name, Amen.

My Commitment

By the grace of God through faith, I will rise above small challenges that try to distract me on the way to my destiny. I will not fear or worry.

Instead, I will embrace these challenges as steppingstones toward my destiny. I commit to continually dwell in God's presence and build my faith in Him by studying the scriptures daily.

CHAPTER TEN

The Horsemen

"Fear none of those things which thou shalt suffer: behold, the devil shall cast some of you into prison, that ye may be tried; and ye shall have tribulation ten days: be thou faithful unto death, and I will give thee a crown of life"
(Revelation 2:10).

When the reward we receive for completing a mission is the crown of life, the road to achieving that mission will undoubtedly be full of tough challenges. These extremely tough challenges are what I like to call "the horsemen" as adapted from the concept of ancient wars where the horse-mounted soldiers (horsemen) were the strongest and most skilled warriors on the battlefield. Like the footmen, the horse riders also represent the trials, tribulations, and challenges we'll face on our journey to destiny.

Let's make a little comparison: Footmen can be compared to our everyday struggles. These may include minor obstacles like forgetting our keys, losing our phone, or running out of milk and having no money to restock. They may not seem significant, but they can still cause frustration and require us to solve problems. On the other hand, horse riders represent more critical challenges that require more effort to overcome. These could include moving to a new city, changing careers, or overcoming a severe type of illness. The challenges may be overwhelming and may instruct us to push ourselves out of our comfort zones and develop new skills.

The Book of Revelation also describes the horsemen as the "Horsemen of Apocalypse." The white horseman is often interpreted as representing the antichrist or false messiah who will bring deception and destruction to the world. The red horseman represents war and bloodshed. The black horseman represents famine and economic collapse. Finally, the pale horseman is associated with death and disease, bringing pestilence and suffering to all those left behind.

Throughout history, the image of horsemen has been used to describe tough tribulations and challenges. In times of war or social upheaval, horsemen have been seen as symbols of destruction and chaos. They are often portrayed as powerful and merciless forces, bringing destruction and suffering to those in their path. Even today, the image of the horseman continues to resonate with people as a symbol of great upheaval and change. From natural disasters to economic crises, the idea of a powerful force sweeping through the world, leaving devastation in its wake, is a potent and evocative image.

However, we should note that footmen and horsemen are essential because they help us grow and become stronger. Footmen may seem insignificant, but they can teach important lessons in problem-solving and perseverance. Horsemen, while more daunting, can provide us with opportunities for growth and personal development that we may not have otherwise experienced. As Christians, we should prepare ourselves to battle with and eventually overcome both the footmen and the horsemen because both will come to bring us down.

When facing and overcoming the horsemen in our lives, faith and spirituality can be significant and influential sources of strength and comfort. Faith is not just believing in our heart that the things we prophesy with our mouth will pass. Trust is also acting like we know we have the strength to overcome, just as young David went up to Goliath, the giant, in battle. We all know the David and Goliath story already, so I need not recount it, but one thing I find intriguing is the conversation between David and Goliath. Goliath said, "Am I a dog, that you come at me with sticks?" (1 Samuel 17:43) and David responded, "You come to me with a sword, with a spear, and with a javelin. But I come to you in the name of the Lord of hosts, the God of the armies of Israel, whom you have defied. This day the Lord will deliver you into my hands, and I will strike you and take your head from you" (1 Samuel 17:45-46).

The level of David's faith was unimaginable; he didn't just have faith, he also had courage, and it was certainly not the courage of a shepherd boy. This is how fierce we are supposed to be when we face horsemen. We must note and understand that David didn't do this alone. In this passage, he clearly stated that he was fighting Goliath in the name of the Lord Almighty, God of Israel. I have just one question for you—Who backs your faith? It's not just enough to believe that we can do something; we also must have the backing that powers us to do that thing and do it efficiently. This brings us to the matter of spirituality.

What is spirituality? Spirituality is the belief in a higher power, a divine force that governs the universe and guides us towards our destiny. It is a connection that goes beyond the physical realm, connecting us to something greater than ourselves. Spirituality is different from religion but can include our religious beliefs and practices. At its core, spirituality is about finding meaning and purpose in life. It is about discovering who and what we are meant to do. Thus, uncovering our destinies in life.

Spirituality can help us cope with difficult times and find peace and happiness. One way to connect with spirituality is through prayer and meditation to God Almighty and with Him. These practices can help us quiet our minds and focus on the divine. Through prayer and meditation, we can ask God for guidance and wisdom and listen for His still, small voice within that speaks to us.

Another way to connect with spirituality is through service to others. When we help others, we tap into something greater than ourselves and feel a sense of purpose and fulfilment. Service can be as simple as a kind word, a smile or more complex, such as volunteering at a charity or community organization.

Spirituality can also be cultivated through self-reflection and self-improvement. When we take the time to examine our beliefs, values and behaviors, we can identify areas for growth and work towards becoming the best version of ourselves. We can also seek out mentors and role models who inspire us and challenge us to be our best selves. The essence of spirituality and its importance is that it enables us to do things that we wouldn't usually be able to do. Just as David wouldn't usually be able to defeat Goliath, he did because he tapped into the spiritual dimension of God's kingdom. We will perform way better than our capacity when we tap into the same spirituality.

However, as Christians, we don't enjoy most of these things and therefore have a much harder time fighting off horsemen because we try to use logic to understand the how(s) of spirituality. We must realize that spirituality defies logic and science from whatever angle we view it. How do we explain scientifically or logically how Jesus was able to turn water into wine? We cannot explain it. It is spiritual and beyond human understanding. 1 Corinthians 2:14 (NKJV) illustrates this better, *"But the natural* (unbelieving) *man does not receive the things* (the teachings and revelations) *of the Spirit of God, for they are foolishness* (absurd and illogical) *to him; nor can he know them, because they are spiritually discerned* (unqualified to judge spiritual matters).*"*

Every challenge we face as we journey to our

destiny can be overcome by reaching a level of spirituality and applying faith. One may say that to be able to do this, we need to read our Bible often and pray consistently at different times of the day, but the truth is that we need to lean on Jesus, listen to His voice and do exactly what He asks us to do. By trusting in Jesus, we can find strength and guidance to help us navigate through tough times. By listening to His voice and following His lead, we can make wise decisions and overcome any obstacle that comes our way. It may not always be easy, but with Jesus by our side, we can have the confidence and courage to face any challenge and reach our desired destination. So, what are we waiting for? Commit everything to Jesus' hands right now.

It doesn't matter how many problem-solving degrees we have or how much of an expert we are. On our own, we still can do nothing. We should take care not to rely too much on our understanding. This should even be intentional. Every time we face a difficult situation, even before figuring out whether it's a footman (small challenge) or a horseman (big challenge), we should call on Jesus and let Him know that we have encountered a roadblock and need Him. If we can make this a daily habit, we will find how calm we will be even in the storms of life. We would start to experience the unique peace that comes from relying on God even when we have no idea what to do; we would still be grateful to God, in faith that He has a plan and that through His program, we would overcome. We should understand that although we can do nothing alone, anything we can think of becomes possible with God.

It can be tough to let go and let God, especially when facing significant challenges. It's natural to want to take control of a situation, to do everything in our power to fix it and make it right. After all, we've been taught that hard work and determination are the keys to success, right? So, simply letting go and trusting in a higher power can be daunting. But the truth is, sometimes, letting God take the reins can be the best thing we can do.

When faced with overwhelming obstacles or situations that seem impossible to navigate, getting lost in the chaos can be easy. We may feel floundering, struggling to keep our heads above water. And that's when it's time to surrender. Now, I know that offering can be a scary concept. It may feel like giving up, admitting defeat. But offering to God is an act of faith. It means acknowledging that some things are beyond our control and that we are willing to trust in a power greater than ourselves to guide us through— sometimes, letting God may mean "doing nothing" to our ordinary eyes. It may seem like we're sitting on our hands, waiting for something to happen. But we are actively letting go of our need to control the situation and allowing God to work in our lives. We are opening ourselves up to the possibility that there may be a better path than the one we had envisioned.

I understand this cannot be easy to embrace, especially if we've always had to do things for ourselves. It's natural to want to rely on our strength and abilities to take matters into our own hands. But the truth is, we are never truly alone. God is always with us, guiding and supporting us even when we can't see it. So, if we're feeling overwhelmed and unsure how to proceed, we can take a step back and consider letting God take over. It may initially feel scary, there is comfort and peace in surrendering to a higher power. We may be trembling with fear at the possibility that everything would crumble if we're not doing something about it, but sometimes the best thing we can do is step back and let God work His magic. Remember, we are not alone on this journey. Some people care about and support us; a higher power always watches over us. So, take a deep breath, let go of worries and fears, and trust that everything will work out. With faith and perseverance, we can overcome any obstacle that comes our way.

My Prayer

Dear God, strengthen me to go through hard times and overcome the trials and tribulations that come my way so that I would wear the crown of life in the end. Help my faith and give me reasons to trust You more and more every day. I understand that there's not much I can do to free myself from life's troubles; give me the wisdom to always rely on You alone. In Jesus' Name, Amen.

My Commitment

I put my faith in God and trust Him to deliver me from the grasp of the horsemen who tried to bring me down. I stay committed to reaching new levels of spirituality and faith in God. I will try every day to make room for Him to take control, and, in the end, I will successfully let go and let God.

CHAPTER ELEVEN

It's a Call to Purpose
and Not Prestige

*"As each one has received a gift, minister it to one
another, as good stewards of the manifold grace of God. If
anyone speaks, let him speak as the oracles of God. If
anyone ministers, let him do it as with the ability which
God supplies, that in all things God may be glorified
through Jesus Christ, to whom belong the glory and the
dominion forever and ever. Amen"*
(1 Peter 4:10-11 NKJV).

What does the call to purpose and not prestige
mean? In Christianity, the call to purpose and not
prestige means that our focus should not be on
seeking fame or recognition but on fulfilling the
purpose that God has given us. This means that
we should not be motivated by selfish desires or
the desire for power but rather by a desire to serve
God and others. We should not do good deeds or

help others to be seen or regarded in high esteem, but rather because it is the right thing to do.

When we seek prestige or recognition for our actions, we do them for the wrong reasons and do not truly fulfil our purpose as Christians. Colossians 3:23-24 (NKJV) says, *"And whatever you do, do it heartily, as to the Lord and not o men, knowing that from the Lord you will receive the reward of the inheritance; for you serve the Lord Christ."* This verse reminds us that our ultimate purpose is to serve God and that we should work with all our hearts to fulfil that purpose. When we do this, we will not seek prestige or recognition but will fulfil our purpose and serve God. This is the call to purpose, not importance. It's in the same way that Jesus was called to save the whole world from sin. His calling came with so much power that people expected Him to be royalty from birth and not a boy born to a carpenter in a manger, but Jesus was disappointed by their expectations from birth, even when He aged. While teaching His disciples, Jesus shared that whichever one of them wanted to be a master would have to be a servant first, which He demonstrated by washing their feet, a task that was usually reserved for the lowliest of servants.

Jesus did not come to this world seeking power

or prestige. Instead, He came to fulfil His purpose. He lived a life of service, constantly putting the needs of others before His own. As Christians, we are called to follow in His footsteps. We are called to serve others and to live a life of purpose. This tells us that, just like Jesus, we should not be focused on seeking titles or positions of authority. Instead, we should seek ways to serve others and positively impact the world, whatever our calling is.

We agree that every Christian has a different calling. Some are called pastors, while some are called to be ministers in songs or even doctors and lawyers. Regardless of the calling, Christians must use their gifts and talents to serve others and glorify God. Each person's unique calling can be a powerful tool for spreading the message of Christ and impacting the world. Pastors play a crucial role in leading their congregations and providing spiritual guidance. They are responsible for teaching and preaching the Word of God, providing pastoral care, and helping people to grow in their faith. However, being a pastor is not the only way to serve God. Musicians and singers can use their talents to inspire others and bring people closer to God. Through worship songs and other forms of Christian music, they can help to create an atmosphere of praise and worship that allows people to connect with God on a deeper level. Doctors and lawyers can use their skills to serve others and positively impact the world. By providing medical care or legal assistance to those in need, they can demonstrate God's love and compassion and help to alleviate suffering and injustice.

I must use doctors and lawyers as an example because some of us have a misguided belief that it is only our pastors and bishops that God calls, and we can do anything we want with our lives because God does not contact us, but that is far from the truth. God has called all of us to be His sons and enter His kingdom. The moment we give our life to Christ, we have accepted this calling and received the primary assignment of spreading the gospel of Christ and bringing people closer to Him. In whatever capacity we may serve or whatever career we choose to follow, we have a primary calling to be a son of God, and we already have a responsibility placed on our shoulders.

I've come to understand that, as children of God, we are responsible for so many lost souls. Through us, generations will be blessed, but what happens when we choose to run away from our responsibility and follow a more accessible road of

91

being indifferent about winning souls for God? We have a purpose on earth, a unit that involves saving lives. Do not just bask in God's glory and enjoy the prestige of being a Christian. That's not what Christianity is all about. Everything that God has blessed us with—the wealth, health, skills, and the rest—is equipment for our purpose, and we'll be doing the world much disservice if we choose not to use these.

God wants us to use our talents and abilities to serve Him. He has entrusted us with His grace in various ways, and our responsibility is to be good stewards of His gifts. As faithful stewards, we must use our God-given abilities to bring glory to Him. We should use our talents to serve others and positively impact the world. Doing so can fulfil our purpose and help us live a meaningful life.

Being a faithful steward of God's grace also means using our resources wisely. Remember the parable of the rich man in Matthew 25 who gave three of his servants different amounts of talents (a unit of currency in biblical times). He gave five talents to the first servant, two talents to the second and one talent to the third servant. The first servant invested his five talents and earned five more, and the second invested his two talents and earned two more, but the third servant buried his talent in the ground out of fear of losing it. When the rich man returned, he called his servants to give an account of what they had done with the talents he gave them. The first two servants showed him the profits they had made and the rich man was pleased, saying, "Well done, good and faithful servant; you were faithful over a few things, I will make you ruler over many things. Enter into the joy of your lord" (Matthew 25:21 NKJV). However, the rich man was angry with the third servant and called him a wicked and lazy servant, taking the talent away from him and giving it to the first servant.

The parable teaches us an essential lesson about stewardship and faithfulness. The first two servants were faithful in using their talents and were rewarded with more responsibility and blessings from their master. The third servant, however, was not loyal and was punished for his laziness and lack of trust in his master. This parable also has a deeper spiritual meaning. The talents represent the gifts and abilities that God has given each one of us. Just like the servants, we are all given different skills and abilities, and it is our responsibility to use them to the glory and service of God. When we use our skills and abilities to serve God and others, we are faithful stewards and will be blessed with even more opportunities to serve and glorify God.

We should also clearly understand our calling and purpose in life, especially as members of the body of Christ. When we know our calling, we can eliminate confusion and find direction in our lives. Our calling is God's unique plan and purpose for our lives. It may involve specific talents, skills, or passions that we have, and it will likely be something that we feel a strong sense of purpose and fulfilment. When we need clarification about our calling, we may feel lost or uncertain about the direction of our lives. We may also be more easily swayed by the opinions and expectations of others rather than following our path. However, when we are clear on our calling and purpose, we can confidently pursue our goals and positively impact the world. This can also help us to connect more deeply with others who share our values and beliefs and work together towards common goals. Ultimately, knowing our calling and purpose can bring greater meaning and fulfilment to our lives and help us live out our faith more authentically and purposefully.

As believers, we may be called upon to lead others we may have once looked up to. This can be a daunting task. We shouldn't be afraid because God has chosen us for this role. It's important to remember that we're not leading people on our own. Instead, we're teaching them through God's guidance. When we lead others, we easily get caught up in our sense of power and importance. However, staying humble and recognizing that we're just servants of God is essential. We receive respect from others not because of our entities but because of the authority that God has given us. As we guide others, it's important to remember that our ultimate aim is to bring glory to God. We should always credit God for our achievements and recognize that all glory belongs to Him.

Answering God's call and fulfilling our divine responsibilities is not always easy, primarily when the world is focused on success and achievement. However, Christians are called to prioritize our purpose over our prestige. We should be willing to lay down our desires and ambitions to serve others and follow God's plan. Many often ask themselves, "How can I fulfil God's purpose?" The answer to this question is not a one-size-fits-all approach. Everyone has unique talents, skills, and abilities that they can use to serve God's purpose. Therefore, it is essential to seek guidance from God through prayer, meditation, and studying His Word to understand His plan for us.

It is also important for our personal growth and well-being to surround ourselves with like-minded individuals with the same values and beliefs. This can provide a support system to help us through challenging times, help us understand and fulfil our God-given purpose, and encourage us to continue our path. A robust support system can help us feel more confident in our decisions and actions. It can be comforting to know that we are not alone in our beliefs and that others are also striving to live their lives in a certain way. We can learn from each other and motivate others to become better versions of ourselves.

Additionally, being around people who share our values can help us stay on track and focus on our goals. It can be easy to get distracted or discouraged when surrounded by people who do not share our beliefs or values. However, when we have like-minded individuals around us, we can hold each other accountable and push each other to stay true to our ideas and purpose.

My Prayer

Dear God, You have given Your children on earth many gifts, and You have given me my gift. Grant me wisdom and discernment, so I may use my facility to its fullest potential, spreading Your love and bringing glory to Your name.

Please help me to understand the true purpose of this gift. May it not be a source of pride or self-centered ambition but a means to serve others and bring about positive change.

Please show me how to use my gift in ways that bring joy, healing, and hope to those around me and help me to remain grounded, always acknowledging that the trustworthy source of my gift is You, my Heavenly Father. In Jesus' Name, Amen.

My Commitment

My eyes will be fixed on Jesus at every point in time, for He is the source of my strength and the compass for my journey. In His presence, I find guidance, inspiration, and unwavering purpose. With each step I take, I will walk in humility, recognizing that my talents are not of my own making but bestowed upon me by a loving Creator. I will remain grounded in the understanding that these gifts are meant to bring glory to God and selflessly serve others.

In the face of temptation and allure, I will stand firm, refusing to be swayed by the lure of fame or the desire for personal gain. I will guard my heart and intentions, knowing that the accurate measure of success lies not in the world's applause but in the transformative impact my actions have on lives touched by the message of God's love.

CHAPTER TWELVE

Journeying Alone

"And you will be hated by all for My name's sake. But he who endures to the end will be saved"
(Matthew 10:22 NKJV).

If we are still scared of being rejected or alone, we're not ready to receive our destiny in Jesus Christ because that's exactly what this journey is about. We do not strive to be loved or accepted in God's kingdom. After all, our Lord and Savior, Jesus Christ, was rejected by His people. Our goal is consistently doing what God has asked us to without seeking human approval. When we decide to follow God and live according to His will, we may face resistance from others who are not on the same path. This is because our actions and beliefs challenge their desires and values, which may be rooted in things not aligned with God's teachings.

People invested in promoting items contrary to

God's word may try to discourage or criticize us for standing up for what we believe in. They see our actions as a threat to their way of life, and as such, they will resist us. It would be best if we weren't surprised many times; the people doing evil will often outnumber those doing good. I'm sure that we all must have experienced this in our lifetime. For example, a maintenance hole has commonly normalized or cheated to get ahead and will often look at us as stupid when we follow the due process, even if they're wrong and right. It would be best if we didn't let that bother us. After all, Jesus said, narrow is the way that leads to eternal life. This means the number of people following that route will also be small. Do not let this be a discouragement. We are called to a unique and particular purpose that doesn't need a crowd to be accomplished. Our friends and family may turn on us when we choose to follow Jesus, but we should remember that all we will ever need in this world we have in Jesus.

It is for the same reason that Job was not broken even when his life told him to curse God and die, and his friends stayed away from him. While the devil thought he was taking everything from Job so he wouldn't survive, Job's everything was God, so he survived. Just as the people around

Job did not understand why he kept trusting God in that state, the people around us may not understand our mission or what we're asked to do. They may also not support our choice of trusting God, but that does not matter. Instead of worrying about their thoughts, pray that God will open their eyes to see and follow Him.

We must be careful not to try to please the world at the expense of our faith. I understand that, as human beings, we often seek validation and acceptance from others, and we want to make everyone happy. However, trying to please the world is sometimes not the right thing. In Matthew 6:24, Jesus warns us of the dangers of trying to play both sides. He says that we cannot stand for God and, at the same time, stand for something else. We cannot have one foot in the world and the other in God's kingdom.

In this passage, Jesus uses a metaphor to illustrate His point. He says that no one can serve two masters. For instance, we cannot serve God and money simultaneously. This is because we will end up loving one and hating the other. Jesus has outrightly expressed that He detests those who are lukewarm. In other words, He dislikes people indifferent or uncommitted to their faith. If we're neither hot nor cold, He will spit us out. He prefers someone passionately committed to their faith or openly rejecting it. It is better to be honest about where we stand than to pretend to be someone we're not. If we are committed to doing God's work or learning to be more committed to doing God's work, then we need to know how to journey alone.

We need to let go of worldly attachments. This is the first step in journeying with God, and it's a decision we must make for ourselves, but it is honestly the best decision. I'm not forcing anyone to make this decision because I know it's one of the most complex decisions they'll ever make. I call it one of the most challenging decisions we would ever have to make because we won't just be leaving the people we love; we will also be going for the things we love, as Jesus shared in the story of the rich man that approached Him.

So, this man comes to Jesus and asks what he needs to do to inherit eternal life. Jesus tells him to keep the commandments, to which the young man responds that he has kept them all from his youth. Jesus then tells him to sell everything he has and give the money to people experiencing poverty and come and follow Him. The young man, however, is unwilling to do so and leaves in sadness because he has many possessions. Jesus then tells His disciples that it is easier for a camel to go through the eye of a needle than for a rich person to enter the kingdom of God (Mark 10:17-22). This story demonstrates the importance of letting go of worldly attachments and being ready to walk alone if one wants to walk with God.

The rich young ruler was unwilling to let go of his possessions and follow Jesus, even though he wanted to inherit eternal life. Jesus knew that his attachment to his wealth prevented him from truly following Him and experiencing the fullness of His grace. Likewise, we must be willing to let go of anything that hinders our relationship with God, whether material possessions, relationships, or habits that lead us away from Him. We must be willing to walk alone if necessary, trusting that God will be with us every step of the way and that the rewards of following Him far outweigh any worldly attachments we may have. And indeed, God will be with us every step of the way as He promised in Matthew 28:20 where He said, "And surely I am with you always, even to the end of the age."

The "alone journeys" with God does not mean that we should seclude ourselves from everyone else and regard ourselves as though we were saints in white and if anyone came close to us, they would stain our white. Don't be the Christian who treats everyone else beneath them just because they believe that they are saved and clean while others are unsaved and unclean. This was the mistake that the Pharisees made in the time of Jesus when they expected Jesus, the Son of God, not to be in the company of unbelievers. Jesus had to correct them, as seen in Luke 5:31-32, when He answered them saying, "Those who are well have no need of a physician, but those who are sick. I have not come to call the righteous, but sinners, to repentance." If Jesus had secluded Himself from everyone else because He felt like He was too righteous, all these people would not have been saved, and salvation would not truly be for all. So, what does the "alone journeys" indeed mean?

Alone journeys mean readiness to leave it all in pursuit of the will of God. This journey is not for everyone; it requires much faith, courage, and determination. We can, however, draw strength from the inspirational story of Moses, who left his comfortable life as a prince in Egypt to lead the children of Israel out of slavery.

Moses was born in Egypt when the Pharaoh ordered all male Hebrew babies to be killed. However, Moses' mother saved him by placing him in a basket and sending him down the river.

He was found by Pharaoh's daughter and raised in the palace as a prince. However, growing up, he realized he was a Hebrew and his people were enslaved in Egypt. He saw their cruel treatment and felt a strong responsibility to help them.

One day, while Moses was walking, he saw an Egyptian beating a Hebrew enslaved person. He intervened and killed the Egyptian. Fearing for his life, he fled to the land of Midian. He lived there for many years, married, and started a family. However, he never forgot his people and continued to pray for their deliverance.

God appeared to Moses in a burning bush and commanded him to return to Egypt and lead his people out of slavery. Initially, Moses was hesitant but eventually agreed to follow God's plan. He left his comfortable life for the second time and returned to Egypt, where he confronted Pharaoh and demanded that he release the Hebrew enslaved people. It was not an easy journey for Moses. Pharaoh refused to let the Hebrews go, and God sent ten plagues to Egypt to convince Pharaoh to release them. Eventually, Pharaoh relented, and Moses led the children of Israel out of Egypt, across the Red Sea, and into the wilderness.

Moses' journey was not one of personal gain or

glory. He left behind his life as a prince and risked his safety to follow God's plan. His journey was one of sacrifice and faith, and he was rewarded with the knowledge that he had helped his people to escape slavery and find freedom.

Our calling may not be saving people from slavery like that of Moses; it may be something smaller or even something more significant. One thing that is for sure is that we will be tested and tried. The road will be challenging. There will be trials and tribulations that will rear their heads at times to challenge us and bring us down, but through all of these, we will stand firm, and just like Mount Zion, we will not be moved.

My Prayer

Dear God, grant me the courage to stand firm in You even if I stand alone. Please help me find the strength to hold onto my convictions, even when they go against the tide.

Please give me the strength to be obedient and follow Your instructions without seeking human approval. Help me recognize that true fulfilment lies not in the support of others but in completing Your purpose for my life. In Jesus' Name, Amen.

My Commitment

I let go of all worldly attachments and lean toward the things of the kingdom, recognizing that my ultimate purpose lies beyond the pleasures of this world.

I recognize that standing for God may not always be easy or popular. Nevertheless, I solemnly pledge to stand firm in my faith, knowing that I am guided by a higher power and supported by a community of like-minded individuals who share my devotion.

I will strive to deepen my understanding of God's teachings and embody them in my thoughts, words, and actions.

CHAPTER THIRTEEN

The Final Welcome

"His lord said to him, 'Well done, good and faithful servant; you have been faithful over a few things, I will make you ruler over many things. Enter into the joy of your lord'" (Matthew 25:23 NKJV).

Have you ever stopped to imagine what your life would be like when God gives you the final welcome? Do you ever imagine the possibility of not being welcomed into His kingdom? What if He says, "I never knew you. Get away from Me, ye walkers of iniquities, for I know you not"?

As a child of God, we should understand that the kingdom of God is our inheritance, and as such, we should not think those negative thoughts—they are only a distraction from the bigger picture. Jesus died and rose from the grave and told us that He has paid for our sins, and upon ascension, He told all of us—every Christian—that He had prepared a place for us so that we would also be with Him. He also told us He would come to take us by Himself, showing us how special we are to Him. It's the same way when we expect a cherished loved one to fly in from another country; we don't just wait for them to come home; we go to the airport to receive them. Even before that, we check in on them to ensure they are still coming and they didn't change their mind. Oh, it's the same way with Jesus.

Right now, He's in heaven, our final home, waiting for us and checking in on us to ensure we don't lose sight of the goal. Like a two-edged sword, He pierces through the deepest part of our soul and speaks to us directly from within. So, why would we ever think that we would not be welcomed into the kingdom He has taken His time to prepare specifically for us? We have an advantage; this kingdom was made specifically for us. God wants to welcome us and it is His will that we eventually get to His kingdom. That's why He helps us get there.

Shortly after Jesus left earth, He sent the Holy Spirit to be our helper, to hold our hands, guide us and teach us His ways. In one way or the other, we may have heard from the Holy Spirit, that still calm voice in us that communicates directly with our Spirit. The one who cautions us when we mistreat someone and the one who says "do this" or "do that" whenever we are confused. He inspires pastors, ministers, bishops, and deacons to speak His Word and will to us so we do not go astray. God wants us, and that's something that I would love everyone to know. And when God wants something, He goes after it; we can't run, we can't hide. He made us and He can always find us if He must.

Remember Jonah? Jonah was one of God's prophets whom He would usually send to deliver His messages to people. One time, God told Jonah to go to the city of Nineveh and preach to the people there, telling them to turn away from their wicked ways. But Jonah didn't want to go to Nineveh. He was convinced that the people of Nineveh would not listen to him and would likely harm him, so he tried to run away from God. He got on a ship and sailed opposite from Nineveh to Tarshish.

God wasn't pleased with Jonah's disobedience and He sent a great storm that threatened to sink the boat. The sailors feared for their lives and started throwing their cargo off the ship to lighten it and prevent the boat from sinking in the storm. All the while, Jonah was fast asleep, comforted by the idea that he had finally escaped God. When the passengers saw that he was sleeping, they woke him up and asked that he pray to his God as they were all doing. The storm was great and knew no calm, so they were convinced that someone aboard the ship was responsible for it, and when they cast their lots, it fell on Jonah. Only then did Jonah tell them who he was and where he came from. They understood that he had disobeyed God, and so they asked Jonah what they should do. Jonah then told the sailors to throw him overboard. As soon as they did, the storm stopped, and a big fish swallowed Jonah.

Jonah prayed to God for forgiveness inside the fish and promised to obey Him. After three days, the fish spit Jonah out onto the shore whole. God gave Jonah a second chance to go to Nineveh and preach to the people there. This time, Jonah did precisely as God had asked. He went to Nineveh and told the people to escape their wicked ways. To Jonah's surprise, the people of Nineveh listened to his message and repented. God forgave them and spared them from destruction.

Through Jonah's story, we can see that hiding or running from God is impossible. No matter how hard we try, God sees everything and knows everything. He always watches over us and waits for us to return to Him.

Whenever we feel like we're not worthy of being welcomed into the kingdom of God, we should read how God transformed Saul, a killer of the saints, into Paul, an avid preacher of the gospel of Christ. Saul was a Pharisee, a religious leader who strictly followed Jewish laws. The Pharisees believed that anyone who didn't follow these laws was wrong and must be punished. One day, Saul was on his way to Damascus to arrest and punish Christians spreading the message of Jesus Christ. While on his journey, a bright light suddenly appeared, and he heard someone say, "Saul, Saul, why do you persecute me?" Saul was terrified and asked who was speaking to him, and the voice replied, "I am Jesus, whom you are persecuting."

The light blinded Saul and he fell to the ground, but he could still hear the voice. Jesus' voice told him to go into the city and he would be told what to do. Saul's companions had to lead him into the city because he was blind. On the other side of Damascus was Ananias, whom God had just instructed to heal Saul of his blindness. Ananias was afraid because he knew Saul's reputation and didn't want to be harmed. But the Lord told him that Saul was a chosen instrument to carry His name before the Gentiles, kings, and the people of Israel. So, Ananias went up to Saul and healed him, and Saul's eyes were opened. He was baptized and began preaching about Jesus Christ. From that moment on, he became known as Paul and travelled throughout the Roman Empire, sharing the Gospel with all who would listen.

Regardless of our religious background or where we are in our relationship with Christ, there is always an opportunity to make a change and begin the journey that will lead us to our destiny and inheritance in Jesus Christ. The first step towards this journey is acknowledging that we need a savior. It is essential to understand that Jesus Christ died on the cross for our sins and was raised from the dead so that we may have eternal life with Him. This means that if we confess our sins and ask for forgiveness, we will be saved, and our inheritance in Christ will be secured. Nobody is perfect and we all have things that we wish we could change or do differently. By recognizing this, we are opening ourselves up to the possibility of a new beginning.

The next step is understanding who Jesus is and what He did for us. According to the Bible, Jesus Christ died on the cross for our sins and was raised from the dead so that we may have eternal life with Him. This means that by putting our faith in Jesus and asking for forgiveness, we can be saved and have a new life in Christ. To start following Jesus, we can begin by praying and talking to God. Prayer is simply conversing with God, where we can tell him about our hopes, fears, and concerns. We can also ask for forgiveness and guidance in our life.

Reading the Bible is also essential, as it is the primary way to learn about Jesus and what He taught. We can start by reading the New Testament, which tells the story of Jesus and His teachings. The goal is to think like Jesus and act like Jesus. The existential "What would Jesus do?" becomes the deciding factor whenever we want to make any decision.

Being part of a community of other Christians is also helpful as we start our faith journey. We can attend a church or join a small group or fellowship of like-minded Christians where we can discuss our questions and concerns with others who are also following Jesus.

It is also essential to understand that this journey will not always be easy. There will be challenges and obstacles, but we must persevere and trust God's plan. He has promised never to leave or forsake us, and He will always be with us as we walk this path. God doesn't expect us to be able to take ourselves to His kingdom automatically, so He sent Jesus to us in the first place. We must understand that eventually being welcomed into God's kingdom is not a function of anything we have done or what we can do but solely depends on God's grace and guidance. Thus, we need to "yield," and we have already done that by surrendering our life to God and following His commandments. Nothing else can separate us from His love and keep us from entering His kingdom. In John 14:6, Jesus made it clear that He was the only way for us to be welcomed into the kingdom of God. He said, "I am the way, the truth and life; no man cometh unto the Father but by me."

God wants us to look forward to getting the final welcome instead of fearing it. We should imagine that He is placing a crown with seven stars on our heads and that we are the happiest we have ever been. Imagine walking on streets of gold and seeing loved ones who have gone before us. Imagine being reunited with our Savior, Jesus Christ, and feeling the warmth of His embrace. Imagine being in the presence of God and experiencing His overwhelming love and peace. But this final welcome is not just a distant dream. It is a reality we can prepare for today. We can ensure that we are pleasing to God by following His commandments and will. We can strive to love others as He loves us and to serve those in need. We may stumble, but we can always ask God for forgiveness and guidance. And as we walk with Him, we can have the assurance that we will hear those precious words, "Well done, good and faithful servant; you have been faithful over a a few things, I will may you ruler over many things. Enter into the joy of your lord" (Matthew 25:23).

My Prayer

Dear God, please give me the strength to go through this journey and be disciplined until the end. Please help me to always remember the crown of life that awaits all believers at the end of our journey. When I am weak, grant me the resilience to keep pushing and trusting in You until I earn the crown of life. In Jesus' Name, Amen.

My Commitment

I commit steadfastly to my journey to God's kingdom, guided by faith and a desire to seek God's truth and righteousness. In all my actions, I will seek to glorify God and be a beacon of light in a dark and troubled world. I will strive to lead a life of integrity, demonstrating God's love through my character and actions.

I commit to building a community of believers with the same vision and passion for spiritual growth.

I commit to nurturing a deep and intimate relationship with God through prayer, meditation, and studying His Word.

CHAPTER FOURTEEN

The Splendors of Heaven

*"In My Father's house are many mansions; if it were not
so, I would have told you. I go to prepare a place for you.
And if I go and prepare a place for you, I will come again
and receive you to Myself; that where I am,
there you may be also"* (John 14:2-3).

When I close my eyes and picture Heaven, I see
the most enchanting place I could ever imagine. A
land of picturesque houses and sprawling
mansions, each more stunning than the last. I'm
sucked deeper and deeper into my thoughts as I
envision Heaven, and it starts to feel like I'm
already there. It fills me with not just wonder but
also hope, and it's not just my imagination that
conjures up this incredible picture of Heaven; the
Bible also does the same.

The Bible speaks of Heaven with such
splendor and beauty that I can almost feel the
sun's warmth on my face and the soft breeze in my

hair. It paints streets made of fine gold and incredible buildings made of the finest and most precise metals. As I dream of Heaven, I know it will surpass anything I have ever seen or experienced. I am convinced that I would never want to leave once I get there. I vow to continue paying the price to get to Heaven: laying myself down, taking up the cross, and following Jesus. Oh dear, Heaven will be so beautiful, and I don't want to miss out for any reason.

Jesus told us that He was returning to His Father's house, Heaven, where He would prepare a place for us. Additionally, Jesus gave us a glimpse into the kind of place He is preparing for us, describing a land filled with many magnificent mansions. Just imagine a place where we can truly feel at home. It's hard to fathom how wonderful this place will be, but I know it will be perfect. So, let's allow our minds to wander and dream of a place where the beauty is endless and the joy is never-ending. A place where love, peace and happiness reign supreme. This paradise awaits us, a place that will make all our earthly troubles seem small and insignificant. A place where we will be surrounded by the majesty of God's creation and be reunited with our loved ones. It's a dream come true, a place beyond our wildest imaginings, and I can hardly wait to call it home.

The apocalyptic book, Revelation, talks in detail about the end of the world and the end of our stay here on earth. In chapter one, we read about how Heaven will be. Verse 23 describes Heaven as a city that has no need of the sun or moon because the glory of God already gives it lightly. There's no worry about night and day or darkness and light, as it is always day and there is always light. This also means that we will no longer be in a dark corner at any time, as the glory of God will lighten up every aspect of our life.

John the Elder, the author of the Book of Revelation, revealed that a river of life flowed from God's throne and on each side of the river stood the tree of life which would heal the nations. Imagine never having to fall sick or worrying about being down in health? That is precisely what Heaven offers to the saints. We will never have to endure another never-ending headache after a tough day at work. It's not just these benefits that we would enjoy; we would also enjoy the physical beauty of Heaven.

John also recorded that the streets of Heaven would be made of pure gold and transparent like glass. Imagine a place beyond our wildest dreams, where the roads shimmer and glow like liquid gold.

With each step, we'd feel as if we were walking on a path of pure magic, surrounded by a breathtaking beauty that would make us forget all our troubles. And it's not just the streets of gold that make Heaven so unique—the roads are also completely transparent, like a window into a world of wonder. As we walk, we'll be able to see everything beneath our feet, as if we were floating on air. It would be a place of incredible clarity and light, where every step we take would bring us closer to God.

The very thought of such a place is enough to fill our heart with wonder and our soul with longing. If I could journey there to experience the joy and awe of such a heavenly realm, I would probably be a trekker or adventurer to discover the paths. It won't matter if I had to walk further than Mount Everest, but I would still try. Well, that's the beauty of God's kingdom and our journey to God's kingdom. We are only required to wait for Him. And while we wait, we should look up to Him in anticipation of God's coming. When we reach Heaven, we will genuinely experience Psalm 16:11 which states that in the presence of God, there is fullness of joy. It will be days, weeks, and months of rejoicing when we reach Heaven. God will wipe away all the tears from our eyes and all the sadness from our hearts. Death will be no more and we will live happily with God.

In Heaven, the promise of eternal life will be fulfilled fully and free of charge. We will also be reunited with our long-lost loved ones who were saved in Christ, and together we will experience the highest glory. God will dwell amongst us and us amongst Him, and we shall sing His praises alongside the 24 elders. Like a newly loved bride in her husband's home, so shall we all be when we get to Heaven. One part of this that I look forward to is the singing. It's already so angelic when the choir sings on earth to God, so how much more angelic would it be when we are singing in Heaven?

But we will never experience Heaven's splendors unless we lay down our lives and follow Christ Jesus. This doesn't mean we must die; death cannot buy us salvation. It means that we must completely surrender to the will of God. This is not just something we do at once; this is something we do continuously. Whenever we wake up, we pray and say, "Not my will but Yours…Lead me, and I will follow…I surrender all to You, God." And then, when we go about our day, we act out everything we have said. Before acting, we would ask ourselves, "What would Jesus do? What would Jesus have wanted me to do? What would Jesus want?" This is the way to Heaven—living a God-focused lifestyle. This way, when we say, "I'm a Christian", we would not be a hypocrite as our Christ-like and God-focused life will show that we're truly Christians.

As Christians working towards making it to Heaven and finally being with our Savior, we should act intentionally through our journey on earth. While we wait until Jesus finishes preparing our mansions in Heaven, we must also prepare ourselves for Him. It's just like in the story of the ten virgins in the Bible. The ten virgins were waiting for the bridegroom to come. They all had lamps, but only five brought extra oil for their lights. The bridegroom did not come as early as expected, and all ten virgins fell asleep. At midnight, it was announced that the bridegroom was coming, and the ten virgins woke up and trimmed their lamps, ready to see the bridegroom. However, the five virgins who did not bring extra oil ran out of oil for their lights. They asked the five other virgins to share some of their oil, but the wise virgins refused, telling them to go and buy oil from the market. While the foolish virgins were gone to buy oil, the bridegroom arrived. The five wise virgins entered the wedding banquet with him and the door was shut behind them. When the foolish virgins came, they knocked on the door, but the bridegroom said he did not know them as he did not meet them when he arrived.

The parable teaches that we must always prepare for the Lord's coming. It doesn't matter that we don't know what time or when. All that matters is that we are sure that He will eventually come, and when that happens, we cannot rely on the faith of others but must have our faith and be prepared to meet Him. Like the five wise virgins, we must have that extra oil for days of unexpected tribulations, or else we would find it hard to overcome them.

What, then, is this extra oil that we must have in preparation for the Lord's coming? That excess oil is the spiritual preparation we need to make a part of our lives and it is a combination of prayer, Bible study and reliance on the Holy Spirit. Prayer is a way to talk with God and seek His guidance and direction. We set aside time to pray regularly, individually and as a community, which is essential. The Bible is God's Word, and it's necessary to read and study it to understand His will and purpose for our lives. By checking the Bible, we can gain wisdom, knowledge, and insight to help us navigate life's challenges. Finally, the

Holy Spirit is God's presence within us, giving us the power and guidance to live according to His will. By relying on the Holy Spirit, we can have the strength and courage to overcome obstacles and live a life honoring God. Combining these three and making them a habit, we can finally experience Heaven's splendors.

My Prayer

Dear God, thank You for creating Heaven for me and sending Your begotten son to show me the way to Heaven. Thank You for Your love and compassion that when I sin, You forgive me and give me another opportunity in Your kingdom. Thank You for the gift of prayer that I can communicate with You while on earth, giving me hope and helping my patience as I wait. In Jesus' Name, Amen.

My Commitment

I commit to serving God truly, embracing His love and living it thoroughly, and being guided by God's wisdom, never straying from the righteous bath.

I commit to sharing the splendors of Heaven with others and wiping away their fears. I'll spread God's message with gentle words and a compassionate heart, igniting a divine spark. I'll seek and embody Christ's teachings, keeping to His commandments in every way.

CHAPTER FIFTEEN

Who Can Understand God's Error?

"Jesus answered and said to them, 'Are you not therefore mistaken, because you do not know the Scriptures nor the power of God?" (Mark 12:24 NKJV)

What is an error? An error is a mistake. We often associate errors with our human nature and have come to understand that errors are a part of us because we are imperfect. But have we ever wondered whether God can make mistakes too? And if He does, can we understand them? Would we be able to point out God's mistakes just as we can point out the mistakes of our friends?

The idea of God making errors is incomprehensible. After all, He is all-knowing and all-powerful and can't make a mistake. But have we ever considered that that could be wrong? We're already thinking about it, and I won't judge because it is very compelling. However, God's "errors," in the sense that many people understand, stem from them being unable to understand God and His Word. This is where many of us get even more confused. We are trying to use logic to understand something beyond our human comprehension. What if we're not meant to understand every decision He makes? We try hard to understand God based on our human logic and intelligence, but God cannot be understood that way. If we keep trying to understand all the why(s) and how(s), we'll never understand God.

God is spiritual and everything about Him is the same. Who can explain how the world came to be? We may only partially grasp the concept of creation. Scientists have their theories about the origins of the universe. The more widely accepted Big Bang theory suggests that the universe started as a single point of infinite density and temperature and then expanded rapidly in all directions. This theory has been supported by a wealth of evidence, including cosmic microwave background radiation, which is the leftover heat from the Big Bang. However, the Big Bang theory only explains some things. For instance, it doesn't account for the existence of dark matter and energy, which comprise most of the universe's mass and energy.

There's also the theory of evolution which is based on the idea that all living things are related through a common ancestry and that, over time, small genetic changes (mutations) accumulate in populations of organisms. Some of these changes may provide an advantage in survival and reproduction, increasing their prevalence in the population. This process of natural selection allows species to adapt to changing environments and ultimately leads to the formation of new species. It then begs the question, why have living things stopped evolving naturally?

The universe is all too delicate not to have a creator. Each creation is precisely placed. Look at the organs in our body. These are things that cannot be replicated. Perhaps the miracle of creation is too complex. Let's consider how Jesus turned water into wine or how He rose from the grave. Can we logically explain that? These are just a few things that people have tried to explain but can never give a logical explanation for. All these things are spiritual, and without divine inspiration, we cannot understand them, no matter how much we try.

Sometimes, bad things happen to us and we want to understand the cause. We feel we don't deserve it and say that God is unfair to us or perhaps He made a mistake. I've been there before and can say that God doesn't make mistakes. Everything happens for a reason, and it's all a part of His divine plan. Others might argue that God does make mistakes, and that's okay. It's not up to us to understand every decision He makes, but rather to trust in His plan and have faith that everything will work out.

Throughout the Bible, there are many instances where it may have appeared as though God had made an error or done something that was not meant to be. One example is when the children of Israel, whom God chose, were enslaved in Egypt for about 400 years. It's easy to understand why one might believe that God had made a mistake by enslaving His chosen people in this way. However, it's important to remember that God has a plan for everything, even if it may not be apparent to us. In the end, the children of Israel were ultimately freed from their enslavement and led to the land that God had promised them, thanks to the guidance of Moses whom God chose to lead His people out of Egypt. This story teaches us that even when things don't seem to make sense or go according to our plans, we must trust in God's plan and have faith that everything will ultimately work out for our benefit.

Just like how the children of Israel were led to freedom despite their hardships, we too can find hope and reassurance that God always has a plan for us, even if we cannot see it.

Even in the Bible, those who believed that Jesus was the Son of God sent to redeem the world from sin must have also felt like God was making a mistake when He let Jesus be crucified on the cross—a most gruesome death. However, the cross was all part of God's plan and Jesus had to be crucified on the cross to fulfil God's will.

When things don't go according to plan in our lives, don't be in a hurry to say or think that God has made a mistake. God is the one who sees the end from the beginning, not us, and He is more interested in seeing that everything works out for us in the future and not just now.

Looking back on our lives, we may often realize that the things we worried about were not worth the time and energy we spent on them. It is easy to become fixated on our plans and desires, but it is essential to remember that God has a plan for us, which may not always align with what we think we want. In times of uncertainty and disappointment, it can be challenging to trust in God's plan. However, the Bible provides many verses that remind us to have faith and trust in

God's plan. One such verse is Proverbs 3:5-6 (NKJV), which says, *"Trust in the Lord with all your heart, And lean not on your own understanding; In all your ways acknowledge Him, And He shall direct your paths."* This reminds us to trust God and not rely solely on our understanding. It is easy to become fixated on our plans, but we must remember that God's plan is always more excellent. By submitting to Him and trusting in Him, we can be assured that He will guide us in the right direction.

I cannot say that we deserve everything that has happened to us because, in all honesty, many things that happen to us are beyond our human comprehension, and often, it has nothing to do with who we are or what we have done. Understanding certain things, like why bad things still happen to good people, becomes draining. The Bible tells us that we live in a fallen world, one that is plagued by sin and suffering. In John 16:33, Jesus says, "In the world you will have tribulation; but be of good cheer, I have overcome the world." This verse reminds us that difficulties and hardships are a natural part of life but that we can find hope and peace in our faith.

Similarly, Psalm 34:19 says, "Many are the afflictions of the righteous, But the Lord delivers him out of them all." This verse acknowledges that even those who live righteously and follow God's commands will face challenges and trials. However, it also reminds us that God is with us through these difficulties and will deliver us from them. It's important to remember that God doesn't cause suffering and pain in our lives. In James 1:13, we are told that "God cannot be tempted by evil, nor does He Himself tempt anyone." Instead, God is a source of comfort and strength during difficult times. Psalm 46:1 says, "God is our refuge and strength, A very present help in trouble." When we turn to God, we can find the courage and resilience to face our challenges head-on.

We may feel it's impossible to say that God made a mistake, but that's what we do whenever we doubt His plans for our lives. Here's why— doubts cause us to feel stuck, and we may start questioning our faith or beliefs. We may even begin to doubt ourselves, our abilities, our decisions, and God's faithfulness. Knowing that trust strengthens our relationship with God, we can already tell how much damage doubt does to our relationship with Him.

I want to paint a picture. Imagine you have a diligent personal assistant who is excellent at her job. Unfortunately, one day, you forgot to tell her about a meeting you had arranged with a client, so she didn't schedule that meeting. You later find out that you missed an important meeting, and you're yelling at her. You start to doubt her competency and fail to believe her when she says she had no idea about the meeting because you didn't tell her about it. By examining her, you are saying that she has made a mistake and has erred in a way. It's the same way when we doubt God. We are saying He erred and made a mistake.

It's like in the Garden of Eden when Eve ate the forbidden fruit and shared it with Adam. Satan had convinced Eve to doubt God's commandment not to eat from the tree of the knowledge of good and evil. He told her that if she ate from it, she would become like God and have knowledge of good and bad. Eve's doubt led her to disobey God's commandment and she convinced Adam to do the same. As a result, sin entered the world, and Adam and Eve's relationship with God was broken. They experienced shame, fear and doubt. They questioned God's love for them and their worthiness to be in His presence. However, despite their doubt, God did not abandon them. He promised to send a Savior to redeem them and restore their relationship with Him. But Adam and

Eve still suffered the consequences of their actions.

We should try to trust God intentionally. Instead of giving in to doubts and questioning, we need to remind ourselves to seek help from God. We can pray, meditate or seek guidance from trusted religious leaders or mentors. We can also read the Scriptures or other religious texts for advice and inspiration. When we seek help from God, we can find the strength and courage to face and overcome our doubts. We can find peace and comfort in knowing that we are not alone in our struggles and that there is a higher power to turn to for guidance and support.

My Prayer

Dear God, please help me to comprehend the depths of Your ways and unravel the mysteries of Your work. Please grant me the wisdom to discern and perceive beyond the limitations of human logic, for Your ways are far beyond my understanding.

I acknowledge that Your existence transcends the boundaries of human comprehension and cannot be confined to logic alone. Please open my eyes to the wonders of Your creation and let me find solace in knowing that Your hand is at work.

May I grow in faith, dear God, trusting that Your ways are higher than mine and Your thoughts higher than my thoughts. Strengthen my resolve to rely on Your divine wisdom rather than my flawed understanding. In Jesus' Name, Amen.

My Commitment

I commit to knowing God by dedicating myself to reading and understanding the Scriptures. I will seek not only intellectual knowledge but also a heartfelt understanding.

I will approach the Scriptures with an open mind and a humble spirit, ready to receive divine revelation and guidance. I will seek God's guidance and illumination as I engage with His Word.

I invite the Holy Spirit to be my teacher, enlightening my mind and opening my heart to divine truths.

CHAPTER SIXTEEN

It Will Be Well Worth It

"Blessed is the man who endures temptation; for when he has been approved, he will receive the crown of life which the Lord has promised to those who love Him"
(James 1:12 NKJV).

Nobody ever said that following Christ would be easy. Even Jesus understood the journey ahead for all those who chose to follow Him, so He spent much time teaching His disciples about the trials and tribulations they would face. Following Christ requires a willingness to put others before oneself. Jesus taught that the greatest commandment is to love God with all our heart, soul, mind, and strength, and the second is to love our neighbor as ourselves. This means that we must be willing to sacrifice our desires and comfort for the sake of others, even if it means suffering or persecution. It also requires us to confront our sins and shortcomings. Jesus called

His disciples to repentance and to turn away from their old ways of life. This is a lifelong process of transformation that requires us to be honest with ourselves about our flaws and weaknesses and to rely on God's grace to help us overcome them.

In addition to personal challenges, following Christ often means facing opposition from the world. Jesus warned His followers that they would face persecution and hatred from those who did not believe in Him. This can take many forms, from ridicule and mockery to physical harm and even death. However, we find strength and courage through our faith in Christ. We find that following Christ is the most fulfilling and rewarding thing we have ever done. Eyes have not seen nor have ears heard the beautiful things that God has in store for those who love Him and follow His commandments.

Through every trial I've faced, I've seen the hand of God working things out. He doesn't fail to prove Himself strong and mighty during the storm. When faced with these troubles or challenges, I often wonder what I would have done without God. It's not only about the tangible things He gives us. Sometimes, we get to experience the intangible blessings of God— things like peace, hope, grace, and love. Money cannot buy any of these things, but God gives it to us free of charge.

But it's hard to believe it will all be worth it when we don't know anything about the future, and it's not just us. Even people who were close to God have yet doubted His promises. An example is the story of Abraham and Sarah. Abraham and Sarah were married and wanted children, but Sarah was barren. God promised Abraham that he would be the father of many nations, but as time passed, Sarah remained childless. Abraham, who was close to God, began to doubt God's promise and questioned how it would come to pass. Sarah doubted God's promise and even suggested that Abraham father a child with her servant, Hagar. Abraham agreed and Hagar gave birth to a son named Ishmael. But this was not the child that God had promised to Abraham.

Years later, God revisited Abraham and reaffirmed His promise to make him the father of many nations. Sarah, now old and past the age of childbearing, overheard the conversation and laughed, thinking it was impossible. But God reminded her that nothing is impossible for Him, and Sarah eventually gave birth to a son named Isaac. Abraham and Sarah's story teaches us that even the closest followers of God can doubt His promises. However, God is faithful and keeps His promises, even when it seems impossible.

We may encounter difficult situations that test our patience, faith, and resilience and wonder why God allows us to endure these challenges before we can experience His blessings. But the truth is, the struggles we face are blessings in disguise. Usually, God prepares us for the benefits He has in store for us. Just like a seed must be planted in the soil, watered, and nurtured before it can bear fruit, we too, must go through a process of growth and development before we can receive God's blessings.

We see many examples of people who went through difficult situations before they received God's blessings in the Bible. For instance, Joseph, the son of Jacob, was sold into slavery by his brothers, falsely accused of a crime, and spent years in prison before he was finally promoted to become the second most powerful man in Egypt (Genesis 37-41). However, through it all, Joseph never lost faith in God and trusted that God had a plan for his life. Similarly, a wealthy and righteous man, Job, lost everything, including his family and health, in a series of tragedies. However, he remained faithful to God and eventually received double for his troubles (Job 42:10). The ultimate example of someone who went through immense suffering before receiving blessings is Jesus Christ. His people rejected Him, He was betrayed by one of His closest disciples, and He was beaten and ultimately crucified on the cross. However, His death and resurrection paved the way for salvation and eternal life for all who believe in Him (John 3:16).

As Christians, we ought to persevere until the end. One of my ultimate wishes is to say, "I have fought the good fight; I have kept my faith." That is what God expects from all of us. Staying strong in our faith can be challenging, especially when facing difficult circumstances. However, there is a greater purpose for our existence beyond this world. We are only here for a moment; afterwards, we will spend eternity with our Lord and Savior. There is pride in knowing that we have walked with Jesus from the moment we heard of Him until He comes to take us to Heaven with Him. The reward is not here; the prize is at the end of the race when we have overcome all the obstacles that reared their ugly heads on our path to destiny. That's where the reward is.

Have we kept our faith? Did we fight the good fight, or were we the loser who ran away, afraid to confront what he should have? I know, in a way, I make it sound so easy but trust me, I know that it is one of the hardest things. I also know that as soon as I lean on God for guidance, it becomes one of the easiest things I've ever done. So, whomever may be going through a tough time right now needs to remember we are not alone. God sees our struggles and is with us every step of the way. He is using our difficulties to shape us into the person He wants us to be and prepare us for the blessings He has in store.

In James 1:2-4 (NKJV), the Bible says, *"My brethren, count it all joy when you fall into various trails, knowing that the testing of your faith produces patience. But let patience have its perfect work, that you may be perfect and complete, lacking nothing."* Romans 8:28 (NKJV) says, *"And we know that all things work together for good to those who love God, to those who are the called according to His purpose."* So, even though it may be difficult to see the purpose in our struggles, trust that God has a plan for our life. Keep the faith, persevere through the tough times, and remember that the blessings after the storm will be worth it. God will guide us in the right direction and use our struggles for a greater purpose.

As the Apostle Paul wrote in Romans 8:18 (NKJV), *"For I consider that the sufferings of this present time are not worthy to be compared with the glory which shall be revealed in us."* Like Paul, we should never forget that our struggles on earth are temporary and will pale compared to the joy and peace we will experience in Heaven. We will no longer experience pain, sorrow, or suffering in Heaven. We will be in the presence of God and our souls will be filled with a sense of fulfilment that cannot be found on earth. Our earthly struggles will be forgotten and we will be free from the limitations and imperfections of this world. Therefore, we should remain steadfast in our faith, even when challenging. We should keep our eyes focused on the promise of Heaven, and persevere through our difficulties, knowing that the price awaiting us is far greater than any struggle we may face in this life.

My Prayer

Dear God, build resilience in me to remain steadfast in my Christian journey. Instill a joyous Spirit within me that radiates hope and love, even in the face of adversity.

Please grant me the strength to endure trials and tribulations, knowing that You are always by my side, guiding and comforting me. Help me cultivate a heart of gratitude, recognizing the blessings surrounding me each day. In Jesus' Name, Amen.

My Commitment

I stay committed to learning from the Holy Spirit, seeking guidance and wisdom in every aspect of my life. I create a space for communion with the Holy Spirit. I strive to deepen my understanding of spiritual truths and integrate them into my daily experiences.

CHAPTER SEVENTEEN

A One-Track Mind to Success

"Do you not know that those who run in a race all run, but one receives the prize? Run in such a way that you may obtain it" (1 Corinthians 9:24 NKJV).

Have you ever competed for something important to you? Or perhaps been around an athlete preparing for a big tournament? You would notice that all they think about is winning. They change their lifestyle, diet, and everything else to increase their chances of winning. They practice to the point that it feels like they're going to break, and it's funny how it is through sweat and panting that they find the strength to pursue their goal and eventually win their prize. But is it only strength that they see? No. They also find their weaknesses. From their preparations, they can already tell whether they will win or lose the tournament.

I admire the most how their shortcomings don't deter them. They keep pushing until they can overcome their weaknesses. They know they are only practicing but run like it's the tournament already. If we don't take away anything else from this book, take this: everything we do while on earth is preparation for the kingdom of God. Whatever is unacceptable in the kingdom of God that we still do here will disqualify us from the kingdom of God. If we must reunite with our Lord and Savior, Jesus Christ, on His second coming, we must live as though we are already with Him. Yes, this is just preparation, but we must treat this time on earth as necessary. If we want to sing hallelujahs to God in Heaven, start now. If we intend to bow to and praise Him all day alongside the 24 elders of the church in Heaven, then we must start now. Preparation doesn't begin when we go to Heaven; we prepare while on earth.

Everyone who wants to win must be focused on doing what they can to ensure they succeed. Another example of this is when we must pass a complicated exam. Even if we have been taught all the necessary information in class, we cannot rely solely on that knowledge to pass the exam. We must put in extra effort by gathering all the course materials, studying them thoroughly, and practicing exam-style questions. By doing this, we increase our chances of success. The same principle applies when it comes to achieving our destiny in Christ. It is essential to have a one-track mind towards our goals and to start working towards them now. This means being focused on doing everything we can to achieve our goals, including prayer, reading the Bible, and following the teachings of Jesus. Just like we cannot expect to pass an exam without putting in extra effort, we cannot expect to achieve our destiny in Christ without doing the necessary work. It's much easier to say "read the Bible and pray regularly" than to put it in practice, but on the other hand, if we don't put these in practice, we can't succeed. So, what do we do?

Jesus has advised us to keep our eyes fixed on Him and nothing else. In Christianity, this is the only track to success, and because of its necessity, He gave us a practical lesson to learn from. We can find this lesson in the Book of Numbers. The Israelites wandered in the wilderness after being freed from slavery in Egypt. They complained about the lack of food and water and even started speaking against God and Moses. As a punishment, God sent venomous snakes among the people, and many were bitten and died. Moses prayed to God for help and God told him to make a bronze serpent and put it on a pole. God also instructed him to raise the bar so that everyone who had been bitten could look at it, and they would be healed. Moses did as God commanded him, and when the people looked at the bronze serpent, they were healed. This was a powerful reminder to the Israelites that they needed to trust in God, even when things were difficult. In the New Testament, Jesus referred to this story when he talked about Himself being lifted on the cross. He said that just as Moses lifted the serpent in the wilderness, He would be raised, and whoever looked to Him in faith would have eternal life. We must fix our eyes on Jesus; the only way to be saved is the one-track mind to success.

As much as we have likened the Christian race to that of an athlete preparing for a tournament or a student preparing to pass a challenging exam, it is not the same. With the Christian race, there's no stipulated timeline. The race is also very different for everyone. For some, it is a short race; for others, it is very long. We know the clock is ticking, but we can't tell if we have ten years to straighten ourselves up and give our life to Christ or just ten hours. One moment we could be partying, and the next, we could be in an ICU fighting for our life.

As we go about our daily lives, we often get

caught up in things that don't matter in the grand scheme. We waste time on trivial things; before we know it, time has slipped away from us. We can't afford to waste any more time. We must decide to turn to Him today, right now. There's no need to fill out any forms or pay any fees. We must approach God, ask Him for forgiveness for our mistakes and sins, and accept His invitation to join His kingdom. Choosing God is the most crucial decision we can make in our lives. It's a decision that will profoundly impact our future in this life and the afterlife. So don't wait any longer. The time to choose God is now, and the way to do it is simple: ask Him to forgive your sins and accept Him as your Lord and personal Savior.

However, we should note that asking God for forgiveness and accepting Him as our Lord and personal Savior is not the end but the beginning. Success in the kingdom of God is repeating this every day and living intentionally so that our life reflects that God is our life's Lord and that He's also our Savior. Living intentionally is more than accepting God; it is also being conscious of our actions and decisions. It means making choices that align with God's will and purpose for our life.

When we live intentionally, our lives reflects God's love, grace, and mercy. When we live intentionally for Him, we become a witness to others. Our life becomes a testimony to God's power and love. We can inspire others to turn to God and experience the same transformation and blessings we have received. Living intentionally for God can help us overcome troubles and reach our destiny. When we make God the center of our life, we gain access to His unlimited power and wisdom. This power can help us overcome any obstacle or challenge that comes our way. So, as we go about our daily day, let's keep our eyes fixed on Jesus. Ensure that our lifestyle and everything else about us prepares us for His second coming.

My Prayer

Dear God, please help me stay focused on my Christian journey. The face of worldly pressures and the pursuit of self-glorification reminds me of the humble example of Jesus Christ, who gave up all earthly riches and willingly embraced a life of sacrificial love. Please give me the wisdom to recognize the emptiness of earthly pursuits and give me the strength to resist their pull. In Jesus' Name, Amen.

My Commitment

I commit to never taking my focus away from the kingdom of God. I commit to seeking His will in all aspects of my life. I desire to align my thoughts, words and actions with the principles of God's kingdom.

Conclusion

We all face difficulties and challenges in our daily lives. From minor setbacks to significant crises, it can be easy to become overwhelmed and discouraged. But I want to remind everyone today that no matter what troubles we face in our destiny journey, they are nothing compared to the joy that awaits us in Heaven. Think about it: the struggles we encounter in this life are temporary and fleeting, but the rewards of eternal life are everlasting.

No matter how difficult our circumstances may be, we can find comfort and hope in the promise of a glorious future with our Lord and Savior. Moreover, these trials and tribulations can work to our advantage. The Apostle Paul wrote, *"...we also glory in tribulations, knowing that tribulation produces perseverance; and perseverance, character; and character, hope"* (Romans 5:3-4 NKJV). When we face adversity, we can grow in faith and develop a deeper relationship with God. So, my fellow believers, let us not be disheartened by the challenges that come our way. Instead, let us take heart in the knowledge that our present sufferings prepare us for a much stronger and more glorious destiny in Christ. Hold fast to our hope and trust in the Lord, knowing He is faithful and true to His promises.

God does not leave us to face our troubles alone. He is there, standing with us during the fire. When we feel like the flames will consume us, we can trust that He will protect us and guide us through difficult times. He is the other man in the fire, ensuring we are not burned. We can face any challenge with confidence and hope when we hold onto this truth. We can be assured that we are not alone and that God is working all things for our good. We may not understand why we must go through specific struggles, but we can trust that God has a plan and a purpose for our lives.

However, God cannot do these things for us if we don't permit Him to, and **we can only help Him by surrendering ourselves to Him**. It's okay to not be in control of our lives and let God, who sees the end from the beginning, take control. We should trust that God has a plan for us, let go of our fears, worries and anxieties, and let God take the wheel. It doesn't mean that we become passive and stop working towards our goals, but rather, we recognize that we can't do it all on our own and need divine guidance and intervention.

However, surrendering to God is not just a one-time event; it's a continuous process. It's about letting go of our ego, pride, and selfishness and opening ourselves up to the will of God. We must actively seek God's guidance, listen to His voice, and obey His commands. This requires humility, faith and patience, as God's plan for us may not align with our desires or expectations.

I keep emphasizing the need to surrender to the will of God because that's the only way we can truly overcome our troubles. When we offer to God, we can rest assured that He will provide us with the strength, wisdom and resources to overcome whatever obstacles we face. It gives us peace of mind and the assurance that we are not alone. We can also grow spiritually as we lean on His divine guidance. It's a way of acknowledging that there is something greater than us and that we are part of a bigger picture. It helps us develop a deeper relationship with God and understand His love, grace and mercy.

This book has taken us on a journey, chapter by chapter, exploring the incredible benefits of releasing ourselves and holding ourselves tightly to

God. **I hope we have all been inspired and uplifted by what we have learned together.**

Perhaps you are struggling with your mental health, feeling overwhelmed by the challenges life throws at you from all angles. If this is the case, I urge you to let go and let God take the reins. Trust that there is a greater purpose and plan for your life and that God is with you every step of the way. There is immense power in surrendering your worries and fears to God and trusting that He will guide you through even the darkest times. By doing so, you can experience peace and comfort that cannot be found anywhere else. So, I implore you, dear reader, to take a leap of faith and let go of your burdens. Embrace God's love and guidance and allow yourself to be lifted and carried through life's challenges. The rewards of such surrender are immeasurable, and I promise you will not regret it. May you find the courage to let go and let God, and may your journey be filled with joy, love and hope.

About the Author

Evangelist Vendrix Headley is a dedicated servant of God who has been preaching the Gospel of Christ for ages. She is also the editor of the "ARYZE" Gospel Magazine, which is a publication that is dedicated to spreading the Good News of Christ to people all over the world.

Vendrix is a loving wife and mother of two sons, Aniel and Nashon Headley. She is a woman who is deeply committed to her family and her faith. Her passion for serving the Lord is evident in everything she does, and she inspires those who know her.

Vendrix was called to be an evangelist at the very early age of eight when she had an encounter with God. Although she was too young to understand the meaning of that special visitation, she experienced a meltdown of her heart with a particular empathy for people. This experience was a turning point in her life, and it set her to become a minister of the Gospel.

Over the years, Vendrix has helped countless people find their way to God through songs and books. Her dedication to her faith is unwavering and she continues to serve the Lord with all her heart. In addition to her work as a minister and editor, Vendrix is an accomplished author uncovering biblical truths. She encourages and inspires others through her books.

Pastor Vendrix Headley is available for seminars, conferences, retreats, and any other speaking engagements. She can be reached via email at aryzenow@gmail.com.

Books written by Pastor Vendrix Headley are available for purchase from her publisher at writtenwordspublishing.com/vendrix-headley, via her personal website at vlove.us, and worldwide wherever books are sold.

Be on the lookout for other books
by Pastor Vendrix Headley:

Swine and Pearls
Smile In the Tears
God's Hurting People (Revised Edition)